THE FINISHED PRODUCT OF HIS FINISHED WORK

Oluwole Otitoola
The Finished Product of His Finished Work

Published by Spines
ISBN: 979-8-89569-721-4

THE FINISHED PRODUCT OF HIS FINISHED WORK

OLUWOLE OTITOOLA

CONTENTS

1. Introduction 1
2. Knowing and Obeying the Word of God 5
3. The Revealed Written Truth 11
4. Lord Jesus' Baptism of John 21
5. The Pentecost 40
6. LESSONS FROM LORD JESUS' TEMPTATIONS 54
7. The Resurrection Day And After 68
8. The New Creation 74
9. The Holy Spirit In-Dwelt And Clothed Believers 94
A Final Note 101

CONTENTS

1. Introduction [illegible]
2. Knowledge [illegible] the Word of God [illegible]
[illegible] Written [illegible]
4. [illegible]
[illegible]
[illegible]
[illegible] 58
The [illegible] 6[illegible]
8. The [illegible]
9. The [illegible]
A[illegible] Note [illegible]

INTRODUCTION

The Lord God Almighty spoke in Deuteronomy 4:2:

"You shall not add unto the word which I command you; neither shall ye diminish ought from it, that ye may keep the commandments of the Lord your God which I command you."

The Word of God is God. According to John 1:1, the Lord Jesus, the Son of God, is the Word of God. John 6:63 states, "It is the Spirit that quickens; the flesh profits nothing; the words I speak to you, they are Spirit, and they are life."

Hebrews 4:12 says,

"For the word of God is quick and powerful, and sharper than any two-edged sword, piercing even to the dividing asunder of soul and spirit, and of the joints and marrow, and is a discerner of the thoughts and intents of the heart."

The Lord God Almighty, our Father, is alive, and so also is His word. Therefore, His word cannot go back to Him void:

"... shall surely accomplish the reason why it is sent," as written in Isaiah 55:11: "So shall my word be that goeth forth out of my mouth: it shall not return unto me void, but it shall accomplish that which I please, and it shall prosper in the thing whereto I sent it."

The word of God is powerful because He is alive. He is the All-Powerful, Omnipotent God, and He will never lie. His words cannot lie. Jeremiah 23:29 says,

"Is not my word like a fire? saith the Lord; and like a hammer that breaketh the rock in pieces?"

The Lord God says of us, His children, that His word, like fire, burns, and like a hammer, breaks and crushes every barrier that may cause or is causing divisions among His children and His church, which He bought with the precious blood of His beloved Son, crucified on the Cross of Calvary. Not only does it cause division, but it also hinders the fulfillment of His will and the accomplishment of His divine purpose for mankind. He made us in His own image and likeness.

Fifteen hundred years after God's great flood, in David's time, King David was giving some advice to his son, Solomon, in 1 Chronicles 28:9:

"And thou, Solomon my son, know thou the God of thy father, and serve him with a perfect heart and with a willing mind; for the Lord searcheth all hearts, and understandeth all the imaginations of the thoughts: if thou seek Him, He will be found of thee; but if thou forsake Him, He will cast thee off forever."

Forsaking the word of God is simply forsaking God, and this is very dangerous because the Lord will cast such a person off forever. King David said in Psalms 27:8-10: "When thou saidst, Seek ye my face; my heart said unto thee, Thy face, Lord, will I seek. When my father and my mother forsake me, then the Lord will take me up."

This means that, with all probability, our earthly parents may forsake us willingly or unwillingly, consciously or unconsciously. But if the Lord takes us up, He forever takes care of those who seek the face of the Lord and obey His instructions.

Our Lord Jesus Christ, speaking from Deut. 6:4 and Lev. 19:18, as seen in Mark 12:29-31, said:

"And Jesus answered him, The first of all the commandments is, Hear, O Israel; The Lord our God is one Lord: and thou shalt love the Lord thy God with all thy heart, and with all thy soul, and with all thy mind, and with all thy strength: this is the first commandment. And the second is like, namely this, Thou shalt love thy neighbor as thyself. There is none other commandment greater than these."

This lets us know that God knows the desires, the thoughts, and the intents of the hearts of all people. He knows those who love Him with all their hearts and those who do not.

Galatians 6:7 says, "Be not deceived; God is not mocked: for whatsoever a man soweth, that shall he also reap."

As God the Father spoke in Deut. 4:2 that we must know and obey His commandments, so also God the Son, our Lord Jesus Christ, is speaking to us by the Holy Spirit in John 14:15, saying:

"If ye love me, keep my commandments." And verse 21 says, "He that hath my commandments and keepeth them, he it is that loveth me: and he that loveth me shall be loved of my Father, and I will love him and will manifest myself to him."

Therefore, in a nutshell, the Word of God, God the Father, and God the Son, delivered to us by God the Holy Spirit, is that we must have (know) and obey (keep) His word (commandment) if we truly love Him with all our hearts.

KNOWING AND OBEYING THE WORD OF GOD

The Psalmist says in Psalm 119:97:

"Oh, how I love thy word (law)! It is my meditation all the day."

The Lord also spoke His word to Joshua as encouragement and as a command in Joshua 1:7:

"Only be thou strong and courageous, and then thou shalt have good success."

Let us see the many benefits of knowing and obeying the word of God, especially as related to the objective of this book. Proverbs 4:7 says:

"Wisdom is the principal thing; therefore, get wisdom: and with all thy getting, get understanding."

The word of God grants us wisdom. The wisdom of God is the most valuable asset in the journey of life.

From Ecclesiastes 9:17-18, we understand that wisdom is better than strength and better than weapons of war. No matter what kinds of battles we are confronted with, with divine wisdom and power, we will surely overcome them all. Psalm 119:100 says,

"I understand more than the aged, for I keep thy precepts."

Summarizing these scriptures, we are advised, or even commanded, that it is very important to know the word of God. It grants us wisdom and eventually gives us strength, which is better than weapons of war. We must endeavor to obey the word of God. In 1 Samuel 2:30, the Lord says, "For them that honor me, I will honor, and they that despise me shall be lightly esteemed." My prayer is that we receive the grace to completely understand the revealed truth, that His light and glory may be upon all who belong to God. In so doing, wisdom shall be exalted, and we shall be able to fulfill the main will and counsel of God for us, His children.

This leads to the second important benefit of obeying the word, especially as it pertains to the purpose of this book.

THE WORD OF GOD GRANTS US PEACE:

Psalm 119:165 says,

"Great peace have those who love your law; nothing can make them stumble."

The peace of God sets the pace for divine intervention. When peace is lacking, destiny is in pieces.

The first thing to do after being born again or regenerated is to seek knowledge. 2 Peter 1:2 says:

"Grace and peace be multiplied to you through the knowledge of God and our Lord Jesus Christ."

The knowledge of God is a requirement for enjoying the peace of God. The level of our knowledge of Him in our lives is directly proportional to the level of His peace we enjoy. As the body of Christ, we are expected to enjoy the peace of the Lord with one another, as one body. When we are at peace with one another, division shall be driven far away from us.

Division in the body of Christ is a manifestation of one of the devil's tactics that robs us of stability.

The will of our Father is for us to battle this issue, so we must confront divisions and deal with them quickly. If divisions creep in, the peace of God will no longer dwell among us.

This leads to the third practical benefit of obeying the word of God.

THE WORD OF GOD DELIVERS US FROM WRONG BELIEFS AND ACTIONS:

Psalm 119:29 says,

"Put false ways far from me, and graciously teach me your law (word)."

There are so many ways now that Satan is using to derail people all over the world, far away from the truth. John 14:6 says,

"Jesus said: I am the way, the truth, and the life; no one cometh unto the Father but by me."

Satan is deceiving many people across the globe, making them believe that there are many ways to the Kingdom of God. This is a lie from the pit of hell. As disciples of Christ and children of God, we have received comfort in this life with immense relief. This is why the Lord revealed this to me by the Holy Spirit through His written truth.

The Holy Bible, which we have been reading all these years, now opens its deeper truth to us. This is not merely an unveiling but a deep revelation of the written word, as presented in the gospel. Over the years, we have allowed the enemy to cause division and carnage within the body of Christ. One faith, one Lord, one baptism—Ephesians 4:5-7. This demonic influence has caused great divisions, so unbearable in some parts that it has undermined the unity brought together by the precious blood of the Lord Jesus.

The Gospel is clear—divisions and baseless claims must be confronted, for they are contrary to the Son of the Living God, Jesus Christ, our Lord and Savior. 1 Corinthians 12:13 and Acts 20:28 speak to this, yet sadly, we have allowed ourselves, as the body of Christ, to be divided further, evolving into different movements and accolades.

It is clearly written for us as children of God. The Lord Jesus Christ said in John 8:32, "And ye shall know the truth, and the truth shall make you free."

The fact that individuals called into ministry are given different messages through revelation does not mean we should become confused or turn them into movements. Revelations to different ministers of God were and will continue to be given for specific purposes. As these ministers focus on their God-given assignments, they receive deeper revelations from the Holy Spirit. 1 John 2:20 and 2:27 remind us that the Holy Spirit is the revealer and the teacher. Let's now read Ephesians 4:1-3.

We are urged to walk worthy of the calling with which we are called, with all lowliness, meekness, patience, forbearing one another in love, and endeavoring to keep the unity of the Spirit in the bond of peace.

However, trying to personalize or, even worse, own these messages has caused conflicts. 1 Corinthians 8:1 says, "Knowledge puffs up, but love edifies."

Most dangerously, the honor due to the revealer and teacher —the Holy Spirit—is not given to Him. The Holy Spirit dwells in us and gives us the things of the Father (John 14:17) to transform us into the image of our Lord Jesus Christ, from glory to glory. Thus, we shall be able to accomplish the purpose for which we were created—to glorify Him.

The apostles of the early church focused on their God-given assignments of preaching and teaching the gospel (the good news) of the Lord Jesus. They made disciples (new converts) greatly and speedily (Acts 2:41-47 and Acts 4:4). They accomplished so much so quickly, despite great opposition and persecution, because they worked together in unity and love. As they did, the Holy Spirit worked greatly and swiftly in that atmosphere of unity and love (Acts 4:29-34).

Sadly, the Holy Spirit is being dishonored by the church today, individually and collectively. This hinders the swift movement of the Spirit, unlike in the early church. We are to be filled with the Holy Spirit and preach the truth (Acts 4:31), for the Lord Jesus Christ is the Truth (John 14:6), the word of God is the truth (John 17:17), and the Holy Spirit is the Spirit of truth (John 14:17). If we preach the truth in truth and with love, honoring the Spirit of truth, the Holy Spirit will glorify God the Son, our Lord Jesus Christ, both in us and through us, as God the Father is glorified in His Son (John 14:13 and John 16:13-14).

THE REVEALED WRITTEN TRUTH

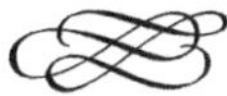

The Conception of John

Reading from the Gospel of Luke 1:5-17, there are two important written revelations we must take proper note of.

Luke 1:5-17

In verse 13, the angel Gabriel first addressed the fear of Zechariah and then comforted him: "But the angel said unto him, Fear not, Zechariah, for thy prayer is heard, and thy wife Elisabeth shall bear thee a son, and thou shalt call his name John."

Let's consider a few things associated with this name, John:

Firstly, the name John came directly from God Almighty through the angel of God, Gabriel, who stands in the presence of God. John is among the selected few names that come directly from God.

Secondly, there had never been any person named John by God before this time. Why is this?

Thirdly, because the name had an important role to play in the plan and purpose of God for mankind by reason of its meaning and the divine timing of God. The meaning of John is: GOD IS GRACIOUS or GRACE OF GOD.

The other name that came directly from God by the same angel Gabriel was the name JESUS (Yeshua), meaning "GOD SAVES or THE LORD IS SALVATION." This occurred exactly six months after John was named by God through the angel Gabriel.

So, combining the two spiritual meanings of the names, we have:

God is gracious, and God saves. Meaning: God graciously saves.

John was the forerunner of our Lord and Savior, Jesus Christ, sent to prepare the way of the Lord (God's salvation) and to make His paths straight. This cry of John was from the wilderness according to Mark 1:3,

"The voice of one crying in the wilderness, Prepare ye the way of the Lord, make His paths straight."

In Isaiah 14:16-18, the scriptures speak of Satan: "They that see thee shall narrowly look upon thee, and consider thee, saying, Is this the man that made the world as a wilderness and destroyed the cities thereof, that opened not the house of his prisoners?"

Satan made the world a wilderness, but John, being God's grace, was crying from the wilderness (the world, Satan's territory) to prepare the way for Jesus (God's salvation).

Why the need for John (God's grace) and not just directly Jesus (God's salvation)?

Since the time God drove out Adam and Eve from the Garden of Eden, the whole world has been in darkness because man sinned. Man, made in God's image, had been separated from God, the Creator of heaven and earth, due to sin caused by Satan's deception.

The same year that angel Gabriel visited Zechariah concerning the conception of John, he visited Mary regarding the unique, unprecedented, and never-before-seen conception of our Lord Jesus Christ. This was around four years before the end of four thousand years from the creation of the earth. It also marked the end of the last four hundred years during which God had been totally silent to the whole earth. These four hundred silent years were a span where no new prophets were raised, and God revealed nothing new to the Jewish people. This time period is referred to as the gap between the Old and the New Testaments, with the warnings from God that closed the Old Testament in Malachi 4:5-6: "Behold, I will send you Elijah the prophet before the great and dreadful day of the Lord: and he will turn the hearts of the fathers to the children, and the hearts of the children to their fathers, lest I come and smite the earth with a curse."

This prophecy is fulfilled in Luke 1:15-17, as the coming of John in the spirit and power of Elijah. The time period also marked the end of about 1,500 years of the law given to the Israelites as schoolmasters (Gal. 3:24) through Moses, marking the era of righteousness by law and ushering in a new dispensation of righteousness through grace. These 400 silent years mirrored the 400 years of the Israelites' slavery in Egypt. Just as the Israelites were in bondage in Egypt without divine intervention for 400 years, so too was the world in serious turmoil during the 400 years of God's silence to the whole world. This was not just a coincidence but perfectly aligned with God's redemptive plan for mankind.

Eventually, the Israelites spent 430 years in Egypt, with 30 years added atop the 400 years. Why? The additional 30 years symbolized the period between the birth of our Lord Jesus and the commencement of His ministry of redemption and salvation for mankind.

The Passover Lamb was killed, and its blood was placed on the Israelites' doorposts during the Exodus after 430 years of Egyptian slavery (Ex. 12:40-41). On the 14th of Abib, around 1446 BC, the bondage of the Israelites in Egypt ended. This foreshadowed the event of the crucifixion of the Lord Jesus, which was fulfilled around 1,530 years later. He was crucified on Passover day, on the High Day of the High Sabbath, as recorded by Apostle John (John 19:31).

John—God's grace crying in the wilderness (Satan's territory) —proclaims in Isaiah 40:1-3:

"Comfort ye, comfort ye my people, saith your God. Speak ye comfortably to Jerusalem, and cry unto her, that her warfare is accomplished, that her iniquity is pardoned: for she hath received of the Lord's hand double for all her sins. The voice of him that crieth in the wilderness, Prepare ye the way of the Lord, make straight in the desert a highway for our God."

Chapter 40 of the book of Isaiah is powerful and revelatory. It clearly shows us the end of righteousness by the law, revealing how terrible and monstrous the sin nature in man is, making it impossible for humanity to fully fulfill the laws. It is extremely difficult, even impossible, for man to keep all the laws; "for whosoever shall keep the whole law, and yet offend in one point, he is guilty of all" (James 2:10).

It was a rough way and crooked paths in the wilderness (the world, Satan's territory), as stated in Isaiah 40:3. There was a need to prepare and make it straight and smooth because it was completely filled with sins produced by the sinful nature in every human being.

Laws, though holy, good, and spiritual, could not bring man to God's order of righteousness because the sin nature in man is terribly sinful—Romans 7:12-14. So, John, God's grace, came to announce (blow the gospel's trumpet) the manifestation of God's grace to end the dispensation of the law for righteousness and bring mankind back to God's divine salvation.

The book of Isaiah closely resembles the Holy Bible in structure. The Bible has 66 books—39 books in the Old Testament (OT) and 27 books in the New Testament (NT). The book of Isaiah has 66 chapters as well. The first 39 chapters of the book of Isaiah, like the 39 books in the OT, are filled with judgment upon immoral and idolatrous people. The law was known for identifying sins and imposing judgment. The OT prophecies also declared the coming Messiah. However, the final 27 chapters of the book of Isaiah, like the 27 books of the NT, reveal that the Messiah has come and emphasize how Jesus, the Messiah, fulfilled the law. The NT declares the message of hope, love, grace, and victorious Christian living by our faith in Jesus Christ, the Son of God.

The 40th chapter of Isaiah reveals the transitional process of the Redemption plan, from the law for righteousness to the dispensation of grace, by which man is redeemed and saved—not by his works, but by grace (the unmerited favor of God) through faith in the beloved Son of God, Lord Jesus Christ. Now, let's look again at the message of God through angel Gabriel to Zechariah in Luke 1:15. Angel Gabriel earlier told Zechariah that the child shall be called John, and they shall have joy and gladness. Many shall rejoice at his birth, meaning that wherever the grace of God manifests, joy unspeakable and gladness shall abound (John 20:20, Psalm 16:11, Luke 1:44, 47, 58).

Angel Gabriel then told Zechariah in verse 15, "For he shall be great in the sight of the Lord, and shall drink neither wine nor strong drink, and he shall be filled with the HOLY GHOST, even from his MOTHER'S WOMB." Why from his mother's womb?

John, meaning God's grace, being the outward expression of God's love or God's unmerited favor, needed a conveyor or a carrier. The only conveyor that can carry the unmerited favor of God is God Himself (Exodus 33:19). He said, "I will make all my goodness pass before thee, and I will proclaim the name of the Lord before thee, and will be gracious to whom I will be gracious, and will show mercy on whom I will show mercy."

The conveyor of God's grace is God the Holy Spirit; He is called the Holy Spirit of Grace in Zechariah 12:10 and Hebrews 10:29. He inwardly convicts with love anyone who has not yet accepted the lordship of Jesus Christ as sinners. When we acknowledge our sinfulness, He convinces us that we cannot redeem ourselves from the power of sin. There is only One—Jesus Christ, the Way, the Truth, and the Life—the sinless, righteous Son of the living God and the ONLY SAVIOR.

"For He hath made Him to be sin for us, who knew no sin; that we might become the righteousness of God in Him" (2 Corinthians 5:21).

God's only Son paid the price for our sins and made us free, for God has forgiven us. Colossians 1:14 says, "In whom we have redemption through His blood, even the forgiveness of sins." Christ brought us into God's light, and though sin is pervasive, many say there are many paths to salvation.

The Living God is clear on this. He created all things in heaven and earth, exceeding human comprehension. Yet, humans made these creatures their gods. Some took mountains, oceans, and rivers as gods, while others worship the sun, the moon, and even stones. Some went as far as calling their god "the unknown god" (Acts 17:22-23).

God, in His mercy and love, has revealed Himself through His beloved Son, Jesus Christ. Yet, many believe that Jesus was just another prophet. However, even their religious texts acknowledge that He was born without sexual intercourse, lived without sin, performed numerous miracles, and rose by Himself on the third day.

One day, the world will recognize the unmatchable Savior who came to free mankind. God has revealed Himself through Jesus. Even Nicodemus, a high-ranking religious leader, acknowledged in John 3:2 that Jesus' works came from God.

The Son of the Living God, Lord Jesus Christ, came in the flesh to be the propitiation for sins, to die for us, and to deliver mankind from sin, Satan, and the world. He rose on the third day to give us eternal life.

GLORY BE TO GOD!

So, John—God's grace filled with the Holy Spirit from his mother's womb—symbolizes the Spirit of Grace.

THE CONCEPTION OF LORD JESUS

Reading from Luke 1:26-41:

Exactly six months after angel Gabriel visited Zechariah, he appeared to Mary. In verse 31, Gabriel told Mary that she would conceive in her womb and bring forth a son and call His name Jesus. Mary asked, "How shall this be, seeing I know not a man?" Gabriel replied: "The Holy Spirit shall come upon thee, and the power of the Highest shall overshadow thee." So, the Holy Spirit here is the Spirit of the Highest.

John 1:14 says, "And the Word was made flesh, and dwelt among us, full of grace and truth."

When Jesus was born, He was fully God and fully man, a mystery beyond understanding. He had no sin nature or original sin.

Leviticus 17:11 says, "The life of the flesh is in the blood." Medical findings show that a mother's and baby's blood do not mix. This proves that Jesus had the divine nature of the Spirit of the Highest, without a sinful nature. John 3:6 says, "That which is born of the flesh is flesh, and that which is born of the Spirit is spirit."

Jesus was born without a sinful nature, as Luke 1:35 states: "And the angel said, The Holy Ghost shall come upon thee, and the power of the Highest shall overshadow thee: therefore also that holy thing which shall be born of thee shall be called the Son of God."

Just as Jesus was born with God's power, so also is every believer born with the power of the Holy Spirit, as we shall see in a future chapter!

LORD JESUS' BAPTISM OF JOHN

According to Mark, the gospel of our Lord Jesus Christ in the first chapter, verses 1-11, reads thus:

Mark 1:1-11.

Let's now look at the meanings of a few names we have in this passage and then apply some substitutions.

God is love, according to 1 John 4:7-8.

Jesus or Yeshua means God saves or God's salvation.

John means God is gracious or God's grace.

Jordan means to go down, run down, or descend.

Wilderness, according to Isaiah 14:17, is Satan's territory, the world.

Verse 2: Behold (Look, See), I (God, Love) send my messenger (John, God's grace) before thy (Jesus, God's salvation) face.

Verse 3: The voice of one (John, God's grace) crying in the wilderness (the world, Satan's territory), John (God's grace) - Prepare ye the way of the Lord (Jesus, God's salvation), make (God's salvation) paths straight. This means we are saved by the grace of God and not by our works - Ephesians 2:8.

Verse 4: John (God's grace) did baptize in the wilderness (Satan's territory, the world) and preached the baptism of repentance for the remission (forgiveness) of sins.

Verse 5: And sinners from Judea and Jerusalem were all baptized by John (God's grace), baptized in the river Jordan (a river going down, running down to descending or pressing down). This means that as they confessed their sins by the grace of God, their sins were washed away, descending (geographically, to where? The Dead Sea).

Symbolically, their sins but not the sin nature were washed down. They were saved but not born again, as were the twelve apostles of the Lord Jesus, including Judas Iscariot. Romans 6:23 says: "For the wages of sin is death, but the gift of God (love) is eternal life through Jesus Christ (the anointed, God's salvation)."

1 Corinthians 15:56 says: "The sting of death is sin, and the strength of sin is the law." Verse 57 says: "But thanks be to God, which giveth us the victory through our Lord Jesus Christ."

This means that sin is a monster and deadly, but the ONLY WAY (not many ways) to destroy it is through the powerful, potent, victorious, and sinless blood of the Lord Jesus Christ, which He Himself symbolically demonstrated and literally fulfilled. HALLELUJAH!

As stated in the previous chapter, grace is simply the outward expression of God's love or the unmerited favor of God, meaning that John here symbolizes God's unmerited favor by the spiritual meaning of his name. Without the Holy Spirit in him from his mother's womb, he would still be limited in fulfilling his divine assignment. John was fully man with the sin nature he inherited from his two sinful-natured parents. But John had two powerful divine assignments to fulfill. His two principal divine assignments for the coming Redeemer are:

1. Announcing the commencement of the new dispensation of grace for the salvation of mankind, and preparing the way to reveal the ONE who would defeat and triumph over Satan and reduce him to nothing.
2. Playing his vital divinely assigned role in God's redemption plan and establishing a pattern to follow for all believers in Christ Jesus, which was first symbolically displayed at the water baptism of the Lord Jesus Christ and literally fulfilled at His Crucifixion and Resurrection.

Without any doubt, for John to successfully carry out these two profound divine assignments, he needed strong support to sustain him. No sin-natured man could carry this role; that is why he was filled with the Holy Spirit while still in his mother's womb (Luke 1:15). Symbolically, he became God, the Holy Spirit of Grace. Luke 1:17 says: "He shall go before Jesus (the Lord's Salvation) in the spirit and power of Elijah." Consequently, John the Baptist was fully equipped for these assignments and symbolically became the Spirit of Grace, empowered like the prophet Elijah.

Now, let's combine the reading of John 1:28-34 and Matthew 3:11-17. John 1:28 says: "These things were done in Bethabara, beyond Jordan, where John was baptizing." This occurred before the remarkable day in verse 29 when John saw Jesus coming toward him and said, "Behold the Lamb of God, which takes away the sin of the world!" Meaning, God's grace sees God's salvation coming to him in the world (the wilderness and Satan's territory). This implies that God's salvation comes through God's grace to sinners in Satan's domain. Behold (see) the atoning sacrificial Lamb of God, who will be killed as an offering to take away the sin (the sin nature, the Adamic nature called the monstrous old man) from mankind - Romans 6:6.

Looking deeply at John 1:31, which says, "And I knew Him not, but that He should be made manifest to Israel; therefore am I come baptizing with water," it is clear that John's purpose was to prepare the way for the Messiah's coming and to make Him known. Why should it be by baptizing Him that He would be made known?

John came as a preacher of repentance of sin, yet he told his followers that they were to look for the pardon of their sins in Jesus Christ and in His death on the CROSS ONLY. God's glory is reflected in pardoning all who depend on the atoning sacrifice of Christ. He takes away the sin of the world; He pardons all who repent and believe in His gospel. This encourages our faith: if Christ takes away the sin of the world, then why not my sin? He bore sin for us on the Cross of Calvary. God could have taken away sin by taking away the sinner, as He did with the old world by the great flood. But He chose another way to remove sin—while sparing the sinner—by sending His Son in the likeness of sinful flesh, as Romans 8:3 says: "For what the law could not do, in that it was weak through the flesh, God sending His own Son in the likeness of sinful flesh, and for sin, condemned sin in the flesh." So, John's testimony concerning Christ at His baptism declared that He is the Son of God, the promised Messiah.

Why should baptizing Jesus with water make Him known (manifested)? It is literal and symbolic. It is literal in revealing what has been foreshadowed and symbolic in bringing to fulfillment what has been revealed.

The baptism of the Lord Jesus in the River Jordan symbolizes God's perfect redemption plan for mankind's righteousness. This pattern stands as an order of God's redemption plan for mankind to follow, as foreshadowed in the Old Testament. The Omniscient, All-Knowing God anticipated conflict in interpreting and understanding His redemptive order for mankind. As God is not the author of confusion but of peace, as in all churches of the saints (1 Corinthians 14:33), He first foreshadowed the order in the Old Testament to be symbolized through Jesus Christ and ultimately fulfilled by Christ and the Holy Spirit in then and now disciples. This is why God fulfilled His Word in Matthew 18:16:

"But if he will not hear thee, then take with thee one or two more, that in the mouth of two or three witnesses, every word may be established."

The plan was first foreshadowed by God through His prophets and priests in the Old Testament. When the Israelites, fleeing from the Egyptians, passed through the waters of the Red Sea, they went from death to life, from slavery to their new lives as God's chosen people (Exodus 14:10-31). Apostle Paul called it a form of baptism (1 Corinthians 10:1-4). Another event occurred in Joshua 3:5-17 when the priests crossed the Jordan River with the Ark of the Covenant, symbolizing a transition into the Promised Land.

Baptism generally means immersion in something, usually water. The key part here is the River Jordan. The spiritual meaning of Jordan is descending or running down. Why was the River Jordan selected for Jesus' baptism? It was symbolically and geographically appropriate—the River Jordan descends into the Dead Sea, the lowest land-based elevation on earth and a place where nothing flourishes, hence its name —the Dead Sea.

In Matthew 3:11-4:1, we read that Jesus (God's salvation) came from Galilee to John (God's grace) to be baptized (immersed into running down) by John (God's grace), who symbolically represents the Spirit of Grace. But John (God's grace) said it should be the other way around, as he felt unworthy to even lace Jesus' shoes. John, a natural human with a sinful nature, empowered by the Holy Spirit, acknowledged that grace should precede salvation.

Grace came before salvation. John (God's grace) was the forerunner of Jesus (God's salvation). John prepared the way in the wilderness (Satan's territory, the world) for Jesus. Ephesians 2:8 says, "For by grace are ye saved through faith, and that not of yourselves; it is the gift of God."

Lord Jesus, fully (100%) God and fully (100%) man, with a perfect understanding of the Trinity's arrangement of God's redemptive plan, told John to go ahead and baptize Him to FULFILL ALL RIGHTEOUSNESS. This means that God has a divine plan to bring man into right standing (righteousness) with Him, and this plan has to be fulfilled. As God is perfect, He expects the redemptive plan to be perfectly followed and fulfilled. This plan was first symbolized in the Old Testament, then literally demonstrated by His Son Jesus Christ, the second witness from the Trinity to establish the truth of God's redemptive plan.

Jesus always sought to do the will of His Father and to finish it (John 4:34). The only one who knows the perfect will of the

Father, Jesus (God's salvation), declared that His baptism by John (God's grace) was to fulfill all righteousness. Jesus, fully man, represented the likeness of sinful flesh but was without sin because the Spirit of the Highest overshadowed Mary for His conception. Thus, Jesus was born without human fatherhood, taking human form through Mary but with God as His Father.

The baptism of a believer in water symbolizes being dead with Christ, and coming out of the water means coming alive with Christ with eternal life, according to Romans 6:3-11. A person needs baptism (1) into the body of Christ, (2) in water, and (3) with the Holy Spirit. God doesn't need any of these; He simply shows us the order to follow.

This means the fully human nature (100%) in the Lord Jesus was symbolically immersed with the fully divine nature (100%) of God in Jesus in the River Jordan (meaning "running down" or "descending"). Who performed the immersion in the River Jordan? John, who symbolically represents the Holy Spirit of Grace, did the immersion, as referenced in 1 Corinthians 12:13: "By one Spirit are we baptized into one body." By one Spirit of Grace, we are united in Jesus Christ's body, whether we be Jews or Gentiles, whether we be bond or free. For we are all made to drink into one Spirit. It is the Holy Spirit who graciously pursues us and convicts us of our sinful and wretched state due to the indwelling of the Adamic sin nature, the old man.

Romans 3:23 says: "For all have sinned, and come short of the glory of God." Romans 7:14-17 states, “For we know that the law is spiritual. Now then it is no more I that do it, but sin that dwelleth in me.” This underscores how terrible the sin nature is in all human beings.

The Holy Spirit of Grace convicts sinners (John 16:8-9) of sin and convinces those willing to listen that they need the Savior —not just a savior. The ONLY SAVIOR is the Lord Jesus Christ (Acts 4:10-12), the only man without sin who lived on earth for 33 years without sin (Hebrews 4:14-15), and who died for all to deliver sinners from the power of sin (Romans 6:22 and Romans 8:2), from Satan (Colossians 1:13 and Hebrews 2:14), from the flesh (Galatians 2:20 and Colossians 2:11), and from the world (Galatians 1:3-5 and 1 John 5:4). He rose on the third day (1 Corinthians 15:1-4) to give us life more abundantly (John 10:10) on earth and eternal life (1 John 5:11-12).

Then, the Spirit of Grace connects willing and obedient sinners to the Lord Jesus, "baptizing" them into Christ’s body (1 Corinthians 12:13).

Ephesians 2:8 says, “For by grace are ye saved through faith; and that not of yourselves: it is the gift of God.”

Now, let’s first see what symbolically happened at Jesus' baptism by immersion in the waters of the River Jordan (running down), and then examine how it was fulfilled physically.

Immediately after John immersed Jesus in the River Jordan, the fully human (100% man) was symbolically buried with the fully divine (100% God) in Jesus. The divine nature of God (sinless) in Jesus KILLED and DESTROYED the sin nature, the Adamic nature, the old man in humanity (symbolically in Jesus' body but literally within us as human beings - Romans 6:1-6). Let's see how the sin nature in man was crucified, put to death, or destroyed.

Leviticus 17:11 says, "For the life of the flesh is in the blood, and I have given it to you upon the altar to make atonement for your souls; for it is the blood that makes atonement for the soul." Simply put, without blood, there is no life; hence, the flesh is dead. The blood of every human has been infected and corrupted by Adamic sin, polluting every human soul with a sinful nature (Genesis 6:5-7 and Romans 3:9-18).

Man is completely separated from God. Romans 3:11 says, "There is none that understandeth, there is none that seeketh after God." Leviticus 17:11, which we read above, states that it is the blood that makes atonement for the soul. Man's blood should atone for sin, but it is polluted. Therefore, sin has been passed down from Adam, making all humanity sinful by nature.

Through the blood of Jesus, who came with the life of God within Him, the sinful nature of humanity was destroyed and KILLED by the divine power in Jesus' blood. Therefore, sin cannot have dominion over a regenerated person.

Romans 6:22 says, "But now, being made free from sin and become servants to God, ye have your fruit unto holiness, and the end everlasting life." This demonstrates that the potent, sinless, powerful, divine blood of Jesus has KILLED and uprooted the power and penalty of sin embedded in the sin nature, the Adamic nature in ALL human beings. Where was it uprooted to? It was rooted out into the Jordan River, which symbolically descends into the Dead Sea, thus flushing the sin nature for permanent WATER BURIAL. This fulfills Micah's prophecy in Micah 7:18-19: "Who is a God like unto thee, that pardoneth iniquity, and passeth by the transgression of the remnant of his heritage? He retaineth not his anger forever, because he delighteth in mercy. He will turn again, he will have compassion upon us; he will subdue our iniquities; and thou wilt cast all their sins into the depths of the sea."

Sin is removed, and the life of a regenerated person in Christ Jesus is established. The Spirit of Life in Christ Jesus (the divine life of God) now replaces the power of sin and death from the old man, making humanity free (Romans 8:1-4).

Let's now see what takes place spiritually in a newly regenerated person according to scripture: 1 Corinthians 6:11 says, "And such were some of you: but ye are washed, but ye are sanctified, but ye are justified in the name of the Lord Jesus and by the Spirit of our God." This means we are washed by the blood of Jesus Christ; we are justified, meaning the penalty of our sin is completely removed, we are declared innocent, and there is no punishment for sins we have committed, including future sins we may fall into, as they are forgiven.

Colossians 2:13-14 says, "And you, being dead in your sins and the uncircumcision of your flesh, hath He quickened together with Him, having forgiven you all trespasses; blotting out the handwriting of ordinances that was against us, which was contrary to us, and took it out of the way, nailing it to His cross." We are made whole and declared righteous. Not only that, we are sanctified, set apart, and made ready for God's use. Sin no longer has dominion over us.

In addition to being washed, justified, and sanctified, we receive the adoption of sons and daughters, becoming the children of God, heirs of God through Christ (Galatians 4:4-7).

2 Corinthians 5:17 says: "Therefore, if any man be in Christ, he is a new creature (a new creation): old things are passed away; behold, all things are become new." We have been made new; the old man, the sinful nature, is done away with, and a new divine nature, Holy Spirit-indwelt, has arrived. We will explore this further in future chapters.

Hallelujah! We are now indwelt with the Holy Spirit. We have become the habitation of the Living Most High God (Ephesians 2:22).

Romans 8:9-10 says: "But ye are not in the flesh, but in the Spirit, if so be that the Spirit of God dwell in you. Now if any man have not the Spirit of Christ, he is none of His. And if

Christ be in you, the body is dead because of sin; but the Spirit is life because of righteousness."

Reading from Habakkuk 1:13: "Thou art of purer eyes than to behold evil, and canst not look on iniquity." How can God, with pure eyes that cannot even look upon iniquity, cohabit with the sin nature? GOD FORBID. God has to kill and bury it. Now, the sin nature has been KILLED AND BURIED. The Spirit of Life in Christ dwelling in the human heart by His divine nature releases His divine power into our human blood, which makes atonement for the human soul, according to Leviticus 17:11.

The life of the flesh is in the blood, and the human soul is the seat of emotion, intellect, and mind. The imparting of divine power from the Spirit of Life in Christ into the human soul is vital and greatly significant.

Glory be to God! We have been made perfect, holy, and righteous positionally by the finished work of our Lord Jesus on the Cross of Calvary. We stand in perfect righteousness and have been seated in Christ Jesus, who now sits at the right hand of the Father in heavenly places, according to Ephesians 2:1-7.

If we've been made seated, perfect, and righteous positionally in Christ Jesus in heavenly places, what, then, is the relevance of Hebrews 4:16 and 2 Corinthians 3:18? This is to reveal to our loving Father how truly and deeply we LOVE HIM through our submission and obedience to do HIS WILL AND PURPOSE, by which we are changed into HIS IMAGE

FROM GLORY TO GLORY on earth. There is a need for us, as newly created, born-again believers, to continually yield to the divine nature and power in the Spirit of Life in Christ Jesus dwelling fully in us.

The more we yield to Him, the more we are transformed into His image. As we yield daily and consistently to the Holy Spirit of Life dwelling in and upon us, His divine presence and power are released in and over our lives. This divine power renews our minds (Romans 12:2), and the mind of Christ (1 Corinthians 2:16) begins to manifest in us. With our minds renewed to the mind of Christ, we manifest transformation and unique, God-inspired thoughts in our lives.

1. There shall be a supernatural manifestation of the Fruit of the Holy Spirit in us (Galatians 5:22-26).
2. We are being changed into the image of our Lord Jesus Christ from glory to glory by the Spirit of the Lord (2 Corinthians 3:18).

2 Peter 1:3 says, "According as His divine power hath given unto us all things that pertain to life and godliness, through the KNOWLEDGE OF HIM that hath called us to glory and virtue."

However, Apostle Peter, by the Holy Spirit, warns us of the danger of not yielding to the Holy Spirit for the working of His divine power in us. 2 Peter 1:9 says, "But he that lacketh these things is blind, and cannot see afar off, and hath forgotten that he was purged from his old sins."

Therefore, there is a need for us to ALWAYS AND CONSISTENTLY REMEMBER what our Lord Jesus did for us on the Cross of Calvary.

Galatians 2:20 says, "I am crucified with Christ: nevertheless, I live; yet not I, but Christ liveth in me: and the life which I now live in the flesh I live by the faith of the Son of God, who loved me, and gave Himself for me."

He loves us undeservedly and unconditionally: "WON'T YOU LOVE HIM?"

John 14:21 says, "He that hath my commandments, and keepeth them, he it is that loveth me: and he that loveth me shall be loved of my Father, and I will love him, and will manifest myself to him."

And to us, His disciples, He said in John 13:34: "A new commandment I give unto you, that ye love one another."

RIVER JORDAN

The Jordan River, meaning "Descending" or "Running down," is a sacred and symbolic river in the Bible, mentioned over 185 times. It plays a very important role in God's redemption plan for all mankind. The source of the River Jordan is the melting snows of Mount Hermon in Israel. According to Google Maps and Wikipedia, it flows down and feeds two bodies of water: the Sea of Galilee at its upper end and the Dead Sea at its lower end. The Jordan River sustains agriculture, wildlife, and trade, symbolizing life and prosperity.

These two seas have significant importance in Biblical history. While the Sea of Galilee is an active regional center of commerce and tourism, surrounded by farms, resorts, and vibrant communities, the Dead Sea is desolate. It is a lake in which nothing swims and nothing grows. The Dead Sea's extreme salinity creates a harsh environment where plants, animals, and aquatic life cannot flourish. Both the Sea of Galilee and the Dead Sea are fed by the Jordan River, but the difference lies in that the Sea of Galilee gives water back to the Jordan River, keeping it full of life. In contrast, the Dead Sea only takes water from the Jordan, making it stagnant and lifeless.

These two bodies of water illustrate a truth about human life: it is through both receiving and giving that life and hope are sustained.

Our Lord Jesus Christ taught His disciples in Luke 6:38, "Give, and it shall be given unto you; good measure, pressed down, and shaken together, and running over, shall men give into your bosom. For with the same measure that ye mete withal, it shall be measured to you again." God Almighty, speaking to the Israelites through Moses—and to us today through the Holy Spirit—in Deuteronomy 15:6-10, says, "For the Lord thy God blesseth thee... and in all that thou puttest thine hand unto."

In other words, the Sea of Galilee acts as a conduit (channel), while the Dead Sea is merely a container, barren and lifeless. Thus, the Sea of Galilee is full of life, while the Dead Sea is full of death. Proverbs 11:24-25 says, "There is that scattereth, and yet increaseth; and there is that withholdeth more than is meet, but it tendeth to poverty. The liberal soul shall be made fat: and he that watereth shall be watered also himself."

Returning to the baptism of our Lord Jesus Christ at the Jordan River, this act symbolizes the greatest gift in heaven and on earth: that the Lord Almighty gave His only beloved Son to redeem sinners from eternal damnation, as written in John 3:16: "For God so loved the world, that He gave His only begotten Son, that whosoever believeth in Him should not perish but have everlasting life." The location of Jesus' baptism was at the lower course of the River Jordan, below the Sea of Galilee. Why this spot? To clearly and undoubtedly answer the question of the sin nature, the Adamic nature, and the old man in the life of every human being.

The prophet Micah prophesied in Micah 7:18-20: "Who is a God like unto thee, pardoning iniquity and passing by the transgression of the remnant of His heritage? He retaineth not His anger forever, because He delighteth in mercy. He will turn again; He will have compassion upon us; He will subdue our iniquities, and thou wilt cast all their sins into the depths of the sea."

Through His divine love, the Lord Jesus Christ destroyed the sin nature in humanity with His divine power and blood, symbolically at His baptism and fully at His crucifixion and burial. The Lord Jesus, by His blood, did not only destroy the sinful nature in mankind but also symbolically purged it out, flushing it into the Jordan River, which descended and carried the sin nature into the Dead Sea for permanent burial.

The Lord Jesus spent much of His life and ministry in Galilee. After His baptism at the Jordan River and His temptation in the wilderness, He returned to Galilee, where He preached, taught, healed the sick, cast out demons, and called His first apostles. After His resurrection, before His ascension, He appeared in Galilee, as He had promised before His crucifixion in Mark 14:28: "But after that I am risen, I will go before you into Galilee." Immediately after He rose, the angel at the tomb told Mary and the other women in Mark 16:7, "But go your way, tell His disciples and Peter that He goeth before you into Galilee..."

Why Galilee? Because He had to fulfill the symbolism of His baptism. Just as He was led by the Spirit into the wilderness to be tempted, so after His resurrection, He returned to Galilee victoriously, having defeated and overcome Satan.

He overcame the world (the wilderness, Satan's territory) for us, fulfilling His words in John 16:33: "These things I have spoken unto you, that in me ye might have peace. In the world ye shall have tribulation (trials and opposition); but be of good cheer; I have overcome the world."

Lastly, He overcame the flesh in the Garden of Gethsemane when He submitted to the will of His Father. After enduring excruciating pain, sorrow, suffering, buffeting, and mockery, He suffered in His body for us.

Our Lord and Savior Jesus Christ returned to Galilee victoriously, establishing the dispensation of grace and defeating the kingdom of darkness. He has inaugurated the Kingdom of God in us and through us to the whole world, as He emphasized in Acts 1:3. This is His heartbeat and should be our passion. Glory to God!

THE PENTECOST

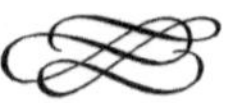

WHAT IS PENTECOST?

"Pentecost" in Greek means "fifty." So, Pentecost day refers to the fiftieth day. In Hebrew, Pentecost is the day of the Feast of First Fruits, observed after seven Sabbaths—forty-nine days. These seven Sabbaths are also called the "High Day" or the "Feast of Weeks," coinciding with the Sabbath of the seventh week. As mentioned in an earlier chapter, this High Day was the day our Lord Jesus was crucified (John 19:31). It was a High Day. Jesus gave up His spirit at 3 PM on Friday, the 14th day in the Hebrew calendar, just before the beginning of the Sabbath, which starts in the evening. This Sabbath marked the start of the 15th day, making it a High Day or High Sabbath. The day immediately following the High Day is the fiftieth day, called Pentecost, or the Feast of First Fruits, which is Sunday. Jesus rose on

Sunday morning, the day of the Feast of First Fruits, as our First Fruit offering. Jesus presented Himself to God, His Father, for our acceptance, symbolizing our total acceptance by God. This means that fifty days later would be another Pentecost, another Feast of First Fruits.

In Acts 1:3, Jesus showed Himself alive after His suffering by many undeniable proofs, being seen by His disciples for 40 days, and spoke of the Kingdom of God. Verses 4-5 say that He *commanded* them not to leave Jerusalem but to wait for the *promise* of the Father: "For John truly baptized with water; but ye shall be baptized with the Holy Spirit not many days hence."

At this point, the disciples were regenerated, born again, newly created, and indwelt by the Holy Spirit. The sinful nature had been killed and buried, and divine nature now fully lived in them. Connecting this with the symbolism of water baptism, this is the moment Jesus emerged from the Jordan River after being baptized by John (the Spirit of grace). The next event was the opening of the heavens and the Spirit of God descending like a dove and resting on Him.

Reading from Mark 1:11 and Matthew 3:16-17: "And Jesus, when he was baptized, went up straightway out of the water: and, lo, the heavens were opened unto him, and he saw the Spirit of God descending like a dove and lighting upon him: and lo, a voice from heaven, saying, 'This is my beloved Son, in whom I am well pleased.'"

Let's first examine the symbolic meaning of God the Father's proclamation over His Son before we consider its literal meaning. This proclamation signifies God's acceptance, affection, and open declaration of His Son in the world, symbolizing Satan's territory. Before this loud declaration, the Spirit of God (the Holy Spirit) first descended on Jesus, signifying the Trinity's united purpose to bring fulfillment in the last days. This mirrors the initial creation in Genesis 1:1.

Approximately 800 years before Jesus' baptism by John in the Jordan River, the prophet Joel prophesied, as recorded in Joel 2:28-32, that "it shall come to pass afterward, that I will pour out my Spirit upon all flesh; and your sons and your daughters shall prophesy… and in the remnant whom the Lord shall call." Apostle Peter confirmed this prophecy's fulfillment on the day of Pentecost, as he preached his first sermon while fully baptized in the Holy Spirit (Acts 2:16-21). Jesus also reaffirmed this promise in Acts 1:4: "And, being assembled together with them, commanded them that they should not depart from Jerusalem, but wait for the promise of the Father… for John truly baptized with water; but ye shall be baptized with the Holy Ghost not many days hence." Thus, in Matthew 3:16, we see "the Spirit of God"; in Acts 1:4, Jesus refers to it as "the promise of the Father"—the Holy Spirit of God.

Let us now look at the resemblance of Matthew 3:17 and Acts 2:6. In Matthew 3:17, there was a loud declaration and announcement from heaven by God the Father concerning

God the Son (Lord Jesus): "This is my beloved Son in whom I am well pleased."

The first event here is the Father's acceptance of His Son, Lord Jesus, and His completed assigned work. This was symbolic and pointed directly to the resurrection of our Lord Jesus Christ, with His resurrected body as the Firstfruit ready to be presented before His Father for our acceptance. He told Mary not to touch Him because He needed (in fulfillment of God's Redemptive plan for humanity) to appear before His Father in heaven as our Firstfruit of the Wave offerings. He appeared before His Father that morning, and His Father glorified Him. He then returned to earth on the evening of His resurrection to His disciples. The significance here is that, no matter how terribly wretched we may be as sinners, once we accept Jesus Christ as our Lord and Savior, God the Father looks at us through His Son and immediately sees us as His accepted children—Hallelujah!

However, not only did He symbolically accept His Son, fulfilling our acceptance with Him; God the Father also symbolically announced His affection for His Son, which was also fulfilled for us when He glorified His Son, Lord Jesus, before Him. Let us see how these truths are established in the Scriptures:

- 1 John 3:1 says, "Behold, what manner of love the Father hath bestowed upon us, that we should be called the sons of God: therefore the world knoweth us not, because it knew Him not."

- Ephesians 1:6 says, "To the praise of the glory of His grace, wherein He hath made us accepted in the beloved."
- 1 Peter 2:9 says, "But ye are a chosen generation, a royal priesthood, a holy nation, a peculiar people; that ye should show forth the praises of Him who hath called you out of darkness into His marvelous light."

If you are reading this book and have not surrendered your life to the Lord Jesus Christ and accepted Him as your Lord and Savior, please don't let this grace elude you or pass you by without responding positively to His undeserved, unconditional, and unfailing love. And if you have already accepted Him but know you have backslidden, please rededicate your life to Him as you pray at the end of this book.

The Lord Jesus, in His unfailing love, has not only made us accepted in the beloved but has also affirmed us as true children of God. Our loving Lord and Savior Jesus Christ did not only appear before His Father in heaven on that resurrection morning with His resurrection body as our Firstfruit for a wave offering but also presented Himself before His Father as our Peace Offering. As discussed earlier, Lord Jesus offered Himself as (1) the sacrificial Lamb, (2) the Priest, and (3) the Offerer of the offering. Hence, God is at peace with us, accepted in the beloved as His children, and we have His peace in us.

THANK YOU, LORD JESUS!!!

Romans 5:1 says, "Therefore, being justified by faith, we have peace with God through our Lord Jesus Christ."

Here are some biblical affirmations for us as children of God:

- I am blessed with every spiritual blessing (Eph. 1:3).
- I am accepted in the beloved (Eph. 1:6).
- I am forgiven (Eph. 1:7).
- I am loved with great love (Eph. 2:4).
- I am chosen (1 Peter 2:9).
- I am sealed with the Holy Spirit of promise (Eph. 1:13).
- I am redeemed from the curse of the law (Gal. 3:13-14).
- I am a light in the darkness (Eph. 5:8-11).
- I am a member of God's family (Eph. 3:6).
- I am Christ's workmanship (Eph. 2:9).

The proclamation of God the Father concerning His Son in Matthew 3:17 was not only for acceptance, affection, and affirmation but also served to symbolically announce to the whole world (the wilderness, Satan's territory) that a new era, heralded by God Himself, had come.

John (God's grace), empowered by the Holy Spirit, had fulfilled his assignment by introducing a new era of grace for God's redemption plan for humanity. He prepared the way for the champion of this new era of grace and made Him known as the Lamb of God who takes away the sin of the world. Having done this, the Redemptive plan and order laid down by God were symbolically carried out by John, as the Spirit of grace, and Jesus, as God of salvation, in the Jordan River (running down or descending), showing it clearly to the whole world (wilderness - Satan's territory).

Now, humanity is baptized (buried) with the God of salvation (Jesus) by the Spirit of grace (John) in the descending waters of the Jordan, with the sinful nature (the old man) killed and destroyed by God's divine nature. The monstrous sin nature is now flushed down into the depths of the Dead Sea for water burial. A born-again, divine-natured, newly created person, emerging alive with God of salvation (Jesus Christ) from the water (fulfilled as the tomb or grave), is now ready to live a victorious, more abundant life on earth and, later, to transition to an eternal home above.

However, because this new person does not immediately transition to an eternal home, they have divine assignments to fulfill as laid down by their Creator (God the Father, the Son, and the Holy Spirit) in the world (the wilderness, Satan's territory). The Creator, following His original plan, saw the need for the newly created person to be sealed (baptized) with the Holy Spirit of promise as prophesied by the prophet Joel about 800 years ago. He chose to symbolize this at His Son's water baptism, for all believers to obey and fulfill His Redemptive plan.

Ephesians 2:10 says, "For we are His workmanship, created in Christ Jesus unto good works, which God hath before ordained that we should walk in them." All believers in Christ have specific divine assignments to accomplish individually, while working collectively as the body of Christ—not in competition but in complementing one another, thereby glorifying Him.

Thus, what was symbolized in Matthew 3:17—"And lo a voice from heaven, saying, This is my beloved Son in whom I am well pleased"—was literally fulfilled on the day of Pentecost in the Upper Room in Jerusalem, as recorded in Acts 2:2-12. After showing Himself alive with many infallible proofs following His resurrection, being seen for forty days and speaking of the things pertaining to the Kingdom of God, Jesus was taken up, and a cloud received Him from their sight. Jesus, now seated at the right hand of the Father in heaven with the Holy Spirit present, reminded and commanded His disciples to wait in Jerusalem to be baptized with the Holy Spirit as promised. So, ten days after His ascension, God the Father and His Son sent down from heaven the Holy Spirit to the disciples waiting in the Upper Room on the day of Pentecost, and they were all baptized with the Holy Spirit of God (the Spirit of Elohim, the Creator of heaven and earth), with fire, receiving the fire-power and dynamite of God.

Now, being filled with the Holy Spirit and fire, they began to speak with OTHER TONGUES, as the SPIRIT GAVE THEM UTTERANCE. The Holy Spirit filled them and GAVE THEM UTTERANCE to speak in OTHER TONGUES. We should not forget that this was a promise of the Father, agreed upon by the Trinity and prophesied by Joel about 800 years before its fulfillment. Shortly after His resurrection, as He commissioned them to go into all the world and preach the gospel to every creature (Mark 16:17), He told them: "And these signs shall follow them that believe; in my name shall they cast out devils, they shall speak with NEW TONGUES." THEREFORE, IT IS VERY IMPORTANT FOR US TO BE IN TOTAL OBEDIENCE TO THE WORD OF TRUTH OF OUR LORD.

The baptism with the Holy Spirit and fire is not only for us to receive power for service but also, as symbolized in Matthew 3:16-17, to announce to the world that we are accepted by our Father and, more importantly, to affirm to the world that the newly created, divine-natured, Holy Spirit-indwelt children of God have come to take over the whole world, walking and functioning in the enormous power residing in us. This enables us to turn the world upside down and bring unsaved souls into the kingdom of our Father, fulfilling His will on earth and glorifying His Son, Lord Jesus. To confirm this, let's look at Acts 2:5-6: "And there were dwelling at Jerusalem Jews, devout men, out of EVERY NATION UNDER HEAVEN" – meaning Jerusalem represented the world, with people of all nationalities gathered there. Thus, Jerusalem was chosen as the place for the inauguration of the Church, marking the beginning of a new era or DISPENSATION OF THE HOLY SPIRIT OF GRACE AND OF POWER (FIRE), showing that the Church was established to go into all the world to bring unsaved souls to the Lord for their salvation.

Now, reading from Acts 2:7-8, we see, "And THEY WERE ALL AMAZED AND MARVELED," and verse 8 says, "And how hear we every man in our own tongues, wherein we were born?" This demonstrates the awesomeness of God in us and the divine power of the Holy Spirit manifesting through us, glorifying God worldwide.

Returning to the baptism of the Lord Jesus, immediately after He came out of the Jordan River, the Spirit of God descended upon Him like a dove. Matthew 4:1 says, "Then was Jesus led up of the Spirit into the wilderness to be tempted of the devil." Verse 2 says, "And when He had fasted forty days and forty nights, He was afterward hungry." Why should the Lord be tempted by the devil? And why should He fast for 40 days and nights in the wilderness instead of inside a house? The number forty is symbolic, appearing around 157 times in the Bible. It signifies periods of trial, testing, transformation, growth, and a change from one era or task to another. A few notable examples include:

In Genesis 7:12, God flooded the earth by sending rain for 40 days and nights, wiping out the first world because "the wickedness of man was great in the earth, and every imagination of the thoughts of his heart was only evil continually" (Genesis 6:5-13). Afterward, God started a new world with Noah and his family because "Noah found grace in the eyes of the Lord," being a just man and perfect in his generation, and he walked with God.

The Israelites, God's people by His covenant with Abraham, lived in Egypt for many years under bondage and slavery. God brought them out and began a new dispensation with His chosen people. He commanded their leader, Moses, to meet Him on Mount Sinai twice, each time for 40 days and nights, to receive His laws. This was the Old Testament/Covenant era, the dispensation of law, lasting about 1,500 years; the first world, from creation to the flood, also lasted about 1,600 years.

Thus, according to His Redemption plan, the Creator of heaven and earth saw it was time to end the dispensation of Law and usher in a NEW DISPENSATION OF THE HOLY SPIRIT OF GRACE. It is unfortunate to hear preachers emphasize grace while minimizing the Holy Spirit. John, representing God's grace, could not have fulfilled his assignment without the Holy Spirit; that is why he was baptized with the Holy Spirit while still in Elizabeth's womb. Just as people in previous dispensations neglected God the Father, and those in Jesus' time neglected Jesus, so too, unfortunately, does the Church often neglect the Holy Spirit in HIS DISPENSATION. I pray that the Church will give God the Holy Spirit the honor due to Him.

Each dispensation, from the fall of man in Eden to the end of the law, was imperfect because imperfect people were involved. The entire world was a wilderness under the control of the "prince of the power of the air" (Ephesians 2:2), the "god of this world" (2 Corinthians 4:4), Satan, who turned the world into a wilderness (Isaiah 14:17), having taken dominion from Adam through deception (Luke 4:6, Romans 6:16).

The dispensation of grace, according to God's Redemption plan, involves a newly created man indwelt by the Holy Spirit without sin nature. Therefore, the Creator Himself had to be involved. The God of Salvation, Lord Jesus, dealt a decisive blow to the old man, the sin nature, killing it and burying it in the depths of the sea, freeing humanity from sin's dominion (Romans 6:6-11). The newly created man, born again and indwelt by the Holy Spirit, is washed, sanctified, and justified in the name of the Lord Jesus and by the Spirit of God (1 Corinthians 6:11). However, this new man must live in a polluted world. Therefore, the Creator has to address both the sinful world and the devil who corrupted it.

The Lord Jesus, God's salvation and a symbol of the newly created man, emerged from the Jordan, symbolizing God's life. The Spirit of God, as promised, descended upon Him like a dove (Ephesians 4:30), sealing Him (and us) until the day of redemption (1 Thessalonians 4:16-17). This was literally fulfilled on Pentecost when the Lord baptized His disciples by sending upon them the Holy Spirit of Promise with fire, evidenced by SPEAKING IN OTHER TONGUES.

Thus, God the Son, along with believers, was sealed and empowered, fully baptized with the Holy Spirit and fire, and led into the wilderness (the world, Satan's territory) to be tempted by the devil. This was THE TRINITY ON THE OFFENSIVE AGAINST SATAN AND HIS RULE, TO

DELIVER THE WORLD. Satan, struck a powerful blow internally, needed to be incapacitated externally. Not only was Jesus (and, by extension, believers) sealed and empowered by God the Holy Spirit, but God the Father also publicly announced the coming of HIS KINGDOM to the world with His beloved Son as the Champion of Salvation, prepared and established by the Spirit of Grace.

This symbolism was literally fulfilled on Pentecost in Jerusalem. The Church of God, represented by 120 disciples, was already made new, born again, and fully indwelt by the Holy Spirit, with no sin nature. Yet, they were commanded to wait for the final stage: being sealed and empowered through baptism by the Holy Spirit, The Elohim, and with fire. THIS COMMAND CAME FROM THE LORD AND CHAMPION OF SALVATION HIMSELF (Acts 1:4-5).

Before His final ascension, Jesus commanded them, commissioning them in Mark 16:15-17, "Go ye into all the world, and preach the gospel to EVERY CREATURE. He that believeth and is baptized shall be saved; but he that believeth not shall be damned. And these signs shall follow them that believe; In my name shall they cast out devils; THEY SHALL SPEAK WITH NEW TONGUES."

This shows that all BELIEVERS IN CHRIST are commanded to be sealed and empowered, submitting to our Lord and Champion for Him to baptize us with the Holy Spirit of Promise from God His Father, with fire, confirming that we are the accepted, beloved, and affirmed children of God.

Secondly, we are fully equipped and empowered WITH EVIDENCE OF SPEAKING WITH NEW TONGUES to go into the world, obeying His Great Commission, reaching the six billion unsaved people in the world. THIS IS WHAT HE DIED FOR, AND THIS IS HIS COMMAND OR GREAT COMMISSION, as He stated in John 14:21: "He that hath my commandments, and keepeth them, he it is that loveth me; and he that loveth me shall be loved of my Father, and I will love him, and will manifest myself to him."

Therefore, brethren, let's set aside any denominational or doctrinal obstacles hindering the powerful move of the Holy Spirit in our lives, reaching out to the world and bringing the unsaved people He died for into His Kingdom, showing our SINCERE LOVE FOR HIM.

LESSONS FROM LORD JESUS' TEMPTATIONS

PRAISE THE LORD!!!

The Lord Jesus Christ has conquered and triumphed over the internal front of the battle. He has symbolically killed the Adamic and sin nature; and the old man has been buried in the depths of the Dead Sea. The external front was next to be dealt with. So, the three persons of the Godhead (the Trinity) went on the offensive in the wilderness (Satan's territory, the world) to expose, cripple, paralyze, and defeat Satan, along with his schemes, tactics, and weapons.

Symbolically, the Lord Jesus reveals to us how Satan operates and attacks humanity in his own territory, the world. Satan hates God and is constantly on an onslaught to destroy anything that belongs to or is instituted by God. Consequently, all humans are Satan's target for destruction. This is a message to anyone who is doing the bidding of the devil and thinks they are prospering—it's a lie. Satan is only preparing such a person for destruction, whether here on earth or eternally. The only one who knows Satan better than Satan himself calls him a murderer, a liar, and the father of lies (John 8:44). Out of love for humanity, God reveals even further that Satan's sole missions are to steal, kill, and destroy (John 10:10). Satan is not a friend to any human, and the only name that makes Satan tremble is the Name of JESUS.

Philippians 2:9-11 says, "Wherefore God also hath highly exalted him, and given him a name which is above every name: That at the name of Jesus every knee should bow, of things in heaven, and things in earth, and things under the earth; And that every tongue should confess that Jesus Christ is Lord, to the glory of God the Father."

Just as our Lord Jesus, symbolizing us as believers, was empowered and led by the Holy Spirit into the wilderness to be tempted by the devil, so are we empowered and sent into the world to confront the devil and bring souls into His kingdom. Satan tempted the Lord Jesus with three temptations, and today, we are confronted with temptations in three main areas: (1) the lust of the flesh (Luke 4:2-4 and Matthew 4:2-4), (2) the lust of the eyes (Luke 4:5-8 and Matthew 4:8-10), and (3) the pride of life (Luke 4:9-13 and Matthew 4:5-7).

After fasting for 40 days and 40 nights to end the dispensation of law for righteousness and to begin the dispensation of grace for righteousness, the Lord was hungry. These 40 days and nights were fulfilled from the day of His resurrection and the new creation of man, His Apostles (John 20), to the day of His ascension, when "He was taken up, and a cloud received Him out of their sight" (Acts 1:3, 9). During these 40 days before His ascension, He spoke of things pertaining to the kingdom of God, bringing into fulfillment His words at the beginning of His ministry in Mark 1:14-15, preaching the gospel of the Kingdom of God.

Now, let's explore the three temptations and understand why He was tempted and how these temptations relate to His Church, His body.

Firstly, God is the Creator of ALL things, including Satan, who was originally created as an archangel named Lucifer (Isaiah 14:12) but became Satan, the evil one, the adversary, the serpent of old, and the dragon (Revelation 20:2). The Almighty God, being all-knowing (omniscient), all-present (omnipresent), and all-powerful (omnipotent), allowed these temptations to reveal Satan's modus operandi—how he deceives and lures people to sin against God, his way of expressing hatred toward God.

Secondly, Matthew 4:1 states that the Lord Jesus was led into the wilderness to be tempted by the devil because it was time for the Lord to strip from Satan the dominion power he had deceptively stolen from Adam. Luke 4:6 records, "And the devil said unto Him, 'All this power will I give thee, and the glory of them; for that is delivered unto me; and to whomsoever I will I give it.'" This was both literal and symbolic—literal for Jesus to fulfill His ministry victoriously (Luke 4:14-19) and symbolic as a revelation for us on how to overcome Satan's temptations.

This victory was later demonstrated on Pentecost when the disciples were baptized (sealed) and empowered by the Holy Spirit's divine fire. This empowerment continues today, as commanded in Matthew 28:18-20: "All authority has been given to me … and lo, I am with you always, even to the end of the age."

In Luke 4:1-13 and Matthew 4:1-11, Jesus faced Satan's temptations: the lust of the flesh, the lust of the eyes, and the pride of life. Glory be to God—our Lord prevailed, defeating Satan! Hallelujah! In 1 John 2:15-17, we are warned not to love the world: "Do not love the world … the lust of the flesh, the lust of the eyes, and the pride of life—these are not of the Father but are of the world. And the world is passing away, and the lust of it; but he who does the will of God abides forever." This passage instructs us to stop loving the world, which here refers to the evil moral system that opposes God and His kingdom.

In resisting Satan's temptations, Jesus not only demonstrated His loyalty to God but also showed what Adam and Eve could not do and where Israel had failed in the wilderness. Jesus is our model. Satan, challenging Jesus' identity and authority, said, "If you are the Son of God …" (Luke 4:3). Intimidation, manipulation, and domination are the three main tactics Satan uses to wage war against humanity. Just as he suddenly engaged Eve in conversation in Eden (Genesis 3:1), Satan attempted to intimidate, manipulate, and dominate Jesus, but this time he met his match.

Jesus did not respond to Satan with His own words but relied on the written Word of God in all three temptations—unlike Eve, who engaged in personal dialogue with Satan. This is a vital lesson for believers: we must hold to the Word of God as our weapon and source of strength when faced with temptation.

Satan is not all-knowing but is crafty, cunning, and swift, always searching for information about our needs and desires to use against us. He does this solely to steal, kill, and destroy. John 10:10a says, "The enemy does not come except to steal, kill, and destroy." 1 Peter 5:8 also warns, "Be sober, be vigilant, because your adversary the devil walks about like a roaring lion, seeking whom he may devour."

Satan observed Jesus' 40 days of fasting and prayer, gathering information about His needs and desires. He knew that after fasting for 40 days, Jesus would be hungry. If Satan cannot tempt us through our needs, he will attempt to exploit our desires. Satan understood that Jesus' primary desire was to establish the dispensation of grace, entrenching the Kingdom of God and ending Satan's kingdom of tyranny and deception. This 40-day period symbolized the Lord's resurrection and ascension in Acts 1:3, where He spoke of things pertaining to the Kingdom of God.

Food, like other human needs, is legitimate and scripturally approved, yet Satan can use even these needs to tempt us and try to steal our identity and authority as children of God. Good examples include Adam and Eve (Genesis 3:1-24), Esau (Genesis 27:1-40), and Nabal (1 Samuel 25:1-43).

In Luke 4:3 and Matthew 4:3, Satan, tempting the Lord Jesus based on His immediate need, told Him to "COMMAND THIS STONE to become bread." Why the words "command" and "this"? Satan knew God the Father as the God of all power and authority, with the ability to create anything at any time. Without a doubt, he assumed God's Son would have the same power and authority as His Father. Importantly, Satan was also constantly reflecting on who the "seed of the woman" would be—the one to crush his head as prophesied in Genesis 3:15. Satan suspected it might be the Lord Jesus after he had observed His 40 days of fasting and prayer, though he did not understand exactly how it would happen.

According to the account in Luke, it seems Satan presented a particular stone to the Lord Jesus, saying, "this stone." Being adept at perverting God's word, Satan may have remembered Psalm 118:22, which says, "The stone which the builders rejected has become the head of the corner." Satan might have pondered whether Jesus was to be the head stone of a corner. But the corner of what? It would be the foundational corner of the Church of God on earth (the body of Christ) and the

Kingdom of God. As Jesus says in Matthew 16:18, "And I say also unto thee, that thou art Peter, and upon this rock, I will build my church; and the gates of hell shall not prevail against it." Peter, whose name means "rock" or "stone" (Cephas in John 1:42), is used here figuratively as the head stone of Christ's Church, with the Lord Jesus Himself as the Chief Cornerstone of His Church, the Kingdom of God on earth.

Ephesians 2:20 tells us that the Church is a grand structure, with a cornerstone that holds all aspects of the building together. The Church was built on the teaching of the apostles and prophets, with Christ as the Chief Cornerstone, on whom all doctrines rest. The Church was inaugurated on the day of Pentecost with divine fire—not in Old Testament times. As the cornerstone of His Church, Jesus Christ provided teachings that flowed through the apostles. 1 Timothy 3:15 says, "But if I tarry long, that thou mayest know how thou oughtest to behave thyself in the house of God, which is the Church of the Living God, the pillar and ground of the truth."

The relationship of the Church with the apostles and with Jesus as the Chief Cornerstone is profound. The calling of the first apostles also holds deep significance:

- Lord Jesus Christ — Chief Cornerstone and Head of His Church.
- Peter (Cephas) — meaning "stone" or "rock," signifying the Church.
- John — meaning "God is gracious."

- James — meaning "follow."
- Andrew — meaning "strong" or "manly."

Combining the Hebrew meanings of the first four apostles' names, we have the phrase: "A STRONG CHURCH GRACIOUSLY FOLLOWING THE CHIEF CORNERSTONE."

Satan, by tempting the Lord Jesus to turn "this stone" to bread, wanted Him to diminish His destiny and purpose as the Chief Cornerstone of God's Church on earth. He attempted to reduce Jesus' God-given destiny of saving the whole world to something needful yet far less significant: bread. Satan was hoping Jesus would turn His God-ordained destiny into bread and consume it, much like Esau did in Genesis 25:27-34. Satan is indeed crafty and cunning; thus, we as children of God must be vigilant and prayerful to avoid falling into his traps.

Satan knew that Jesus is the Bread of Life, and whoever comes to Him will never hunger, and whoever believes in Him will never thirst. Yet, he sought to cause Jesus to turn His glory into shame by reducing His authority and destiny to mere bread. If destiny is sacrificed, purpose becomes meaningless. This principle is highlighted by Jesus in Matthew 7:21-28: "Not everyone that saith unto me, Lord, Lord shall enter the Kingdom of heaven … and great was the fall of it."

Dear brothers and sisters, let us continue to hold on to our anchor of hope in God, watching and praying. We are indeed born again of the Spirit of Life in Christ, redeemed by His precious, sinless blood shed on the cross. Jesus did the hardest part by laying down His divine life for us, leaving us the simplest response: to accept His love and receive Him as our Lord and Savior. The only solution to the devil's onslaught is the Blood of Jesus—nothing more, nothing less. Revelation 12:11 says, "And they overcame him by the blood of the Lamb, and by the word of their testimony; and they loved not their lives unto the death."

Satan eavesdropped on the Lord Jesus' forty days of fasting and prayer, realizing that there was a serious threat to his 4,000-year-old kingdom. Jesus, the seed of the woman, was there to crush the head of the serpent and, as Chief Cornerstone, had been fully prepared and empowered by the Holy Spirit to demonstrate for us how to overcome every temptation and live victoriously.

The Lord Jesus responded to Satan's challenge in Luke 4:4: "And Jesus answered him, saying, It is written, That man shall not live by bread alone but by every word of God." Jesus showed that although food was necessary, His Father's will was paramount. To teach this further, He demonstrated His commitment in John 4:31-38 and John 6:35-40. John 4:34 reads, "Jesus saith unto them, My meat is to do the will of Him that sent me, and to finish His work." John 6:38 says, "For I came down from heaven, not to do my own will, but the will of Him that sent me."

Satan was tempting Jesus to perform miracles outside His Father's will. Jesus explained that it is not bread that sustains life, but rather God Himself. The Father's will was for Him to finish the kingdom work by bringing a great harvest of unsaved souls into God's Kingdom. Every true child of God should therefore honor the Holy Spirit, submitting to His power, and strive to bring in the harvest of over six billion souls in need of salvation worldwide.

May the Lord help us to submit and obey, in Jesus' name. Amen!

Satan, realizing he could not steal the identity of the Chief Cornerstone or prevent the Seed of the woman from crushing his head, next tried to tempt Jesus through the lust of the eyes. In Luke 4:5-7, we read, "Then the devil, taking him up on a high mountain, showed him all the kingdoms of the world in a moment of time. And the devil said to Him, 'All this authority I will give You, and their glory; for this has been delivered to me, and I will give it to whomever I wish. Therefore, if You will worship before me, all will be Yours.'"

In Luke 4:8, "And Jesus answered and said to him, 'Get thee behind me, Satan! For it is written, you shall worship the Lord your God, and Him only you shall serve.'"

Satan said, "All this authority has been delivered to me and I will give it to whomever worships me." Who delivered the authority to him? The fall of Adam to the hands of Satan in the Garden of Eden caused Adam to lose his legal right of dominion over the earth to the devil (2 Corinthians 4:3-4 and Romans 6:16).

This temptation was an attempt to offer the Lord Jesus power by wrongful means. Satan's approach involved a detour from the cross (the crucifixion ahead), persuading Jesus to take an easy path to power. Satan was essentially offering a crown without the cross to the Lord Jesus.

Satan, who had rebelled against God by trying to seize worship that belongs to the Most High alone, lost his place and position in heaven. In the same way, he wanted the Lord Jesus to act on His own will, deceiving Him into focusing on worldly things and thus leading Him into the sin of rebellion and disobedience against His Father. This temptation aimed to separate Jesus from the Father's will and glory, which He would achieve through obedience. Symbolically, this shows us the devil's tactics and teaches us to walk in the victories Jesus has accomplished for us. Satan's ultimate intention is to kill us spiritually (by separating us from the will of God, our Father), deceiving us into loving worldly things and abandoning heavenly things, which is simply called "the lust of the eyes." A prime example of this is King Saul in 1 Samuel 15:1-34.

Satan met his defeat again. Unable to steal the authority and identity of the Lord Jesus in his first temptation, and failing again to separate Jesus from the Father's will in the second temptation, Satan moved on to his third attempt. Here we learn another important lesson: Satan is persistent and won't easily leave his target. This is why we must consistently focus our gaze on our Captain, our Champion—the Lord Jesus, the Author and Finisher of faith—and pray ceaselessly, using His powerful blood as our defense (Matthew 26:41 and Revelation 12:11).

Realizing he was losing the battle, Satan became subtler, more compelling, and aggressive, introducing the sin of pride—the pride of life. Satan knew it was this same sin of pride that led to his own downfall and eternal condemnation (Isaiah 14:12-15).

In Luke 4:9-11, "And he brought Him to Jerusalem, set Him on a pinnacle of the temple, and said unto Him, 'If thou be the Son of God, cast thyself down from hence; for it is written, He shall give His angels charge over thee, to keep thee: and in their hands they shall bear thee up, lest at any time thou dash thy foot against a stone.'"

In quoting Psalm 91:11-12 as a promise of protection, Satan manipulatively left out "to keep you in all your ways." Satan is indeed a liar and the father of lies (John 8:44). He tempted the Lord Jesus to gain public attention and receive fleshly glory from men rather than glorifying the Father. This temptation would have had Jesus acting in His own will, seeking glory from men, and ignoring the will of His Father. Satan omitted the phrase "to keep you in all your ways" because he hates God and always tries to diminish God's goodness, focusing instead on judgment before humans.

In Luke 4:12, "And Jesus answered and said to him, 'It has been said, You shall not tempt the Lord your God.'" God may test His children, but they must not test Him through rebellion or sin, as the Israelites did at Massah (Exodus 17:1-7). A good example is found in Luke 9:51-56; James and John, the "sons of thunder," wanted Jesus to call down fire from heaven on the Samaritan villages that refused His message, just as Elijah did (2 Kings 1:9-16). But Jesus rebuked them sharply, reminding them of His loving mission to save mankind. In John 17:1-5, nearing the end of His mission on earth, Jesus asked the Father to glorify Him so that His mission to the world would be made known through His crucifixion. The purpose of this was twofold: first, that the Son on the cross would reveal the Father's love and justice, and second, that through Jesus' death, God would provide forgiveness of sins and grant eternal life to all who believe in Him.

Jesus stated that He glorified His Father by making Him known to the world and by finishing the work God gave Him to do, which was the Father's will (John 4:31-38).

Satan knows why God made man in His own image:

1. To please Him by doing His will (2 Corinthians 5:9-10; Psalm 147:11-12)
2. To glorify Him entirely (Isaiah 6:3; Romans 11:31; John 15:8)
3. To honor Him through worship (Deuteronomy 6:10-28; John 4:23)

4. To bring Him pleasure by loving Him (Revelation 4:11; 1 John 5:3)

For these reasons, Satan is determined to prevent us, the children of God, from fulfilling these purposes for our Father.

Therefore, Satan constantly schemes to:

1. Intimidate us so we displease God.
2. Manipulate us so we fail to glorify God.
3. Dominate and control us, keeping us from loving and worshiping our Father.

THE RESURRECTION DAY AND AFTER

Reading the Gospel of the Lord Jesus in John 20:1-31, in verses 16-17, "Jesus saith unto her, Mary. She turned herself, and saith unto Him, Rabboni, which is to say Master." Jesus saith unto her, "Touch me not: for I am not yet ASCENDED TO MY FATHER: but go to my brethren, and say unto them I ascend unto my Father, and your Father and to my God and your God."

The Lord Jesus is our FIRSTFRUIT, who waved Himself for us to be accepted before the Lord, His Father, and our Father. That is why He told Mary not to touch Him because He had not yet ascended to His Father to present Himself as the first-fruit for our acceptance. Remember, this happened on Sunday, the morning of the 16th day, which was the Resurrection morning of our Lord Jesus. Also, this 16th day was the Feast of the Firstfruits and the day of Pentecost.

In verse 19, we see what happened: "Then the same day at evening (sunset on Sunday), being the first day of the week, when the doors were shut where the disciples were assembled for fear of the Jews, came Lord Jesus and stood in the midst, and saith unto them, peace be unto you." This happened on the day our Lord resurrected, but after He had appeared before His Father, presenting Himself as the FIRSTFRUIT for our acceptance. To verify this, as the Way, the Truth, and the Life, He showed them His hands and His side. Then, they were glad when they saw the Lord. In verse 21, He pronounced peace upon them again and then commissioned them to witness Him and bring disciples into the Kingdom of God. Now, in verse 22, He breathed on them. Why did He breathe on them? He had not done this in the three years they were with Him; He only gave them power to heal the sick, cast out devils, and declare to people, "The Kingdom of God is come near unto you" (Luke 10:9).

Firstly, why did He pronounce peace upon them twice? In Luke 10, He sent out the 70 He had just appointed and told them in verse 5, "And unto whatsoever house ye enter, first say, peace be to this house." Among all the offerings in the Old Testament, the sin offering and the trespass offering were the most familiar due to their close relationship with the crucifixion. The "peace" offering, however, is not only less understood but is also symbolic; peace, experientially, is one of the most challenging aspects of life to practice.

Hebrews 12:14 says, "Follow peace with all men and holiness without which no man shall see the Lord." Romans 12:18

says, "If it is possible, as much as lieth in you, live peacefully with all men." The word "follow" is written in other Bible versions as "strive" or "make every effort," emphasizing the difficulty of practicing peace in life. Let's now examine why the peace offering is so symbolic.

From Leviticus 3:1-5, verse 5 shows us an aspect of the sacrifice that illustrates its purpose. It is burnt after the burnt and meal offerings have been finished, in this order: burnt offering first, followed by the meal offering, then the peace offering. We also see that it is a sweet aroma offering, meaning no sin is involved, and it is most satisfying to God. The peace offering had to be offered after the first two offerings while the fire on the altar was still burning. It is a sweet-smelling and satisfying offering to God. Likewise, the priest receiving his portion symbolizes satisfaction, and the offerer of the offering with his portion is also satisfied. The symbolism is that all three parties involved were filled, supplied, contented, and pleased. In this offering, Christ our Lord clearly plays all three parts: (i) He is the offering being sacrificed, (ii) He is the priest serving mankind at the altar as the mediator, and (iii) He is the offerer bringing His sacrifice to the altar. The altar, as the place of meeting for all three, represents sacrificial service and devotion to God that gives Him satisfaction and results in our acceptance.

In Isaiah 9:6, the Lord Jesus is called the Prince of Peace. He is also the Giver of peace. Isaiah 53:5b says, "The chastisement of our peace was upon Him." Isaiah 26:3 says, "Thou wilt keep him in perfect peace, whose mind is stayed on thee because he trusts in thee." When we rest our faith in the Lord Jesus and trust in Him, His peace fully flows unto us. HALLELUJAH!

Romans 5:1 says, "Therefore being justified by faith, we have peace with God through our Lord Jesus Christ." Job 22:21 says, "Acquaint now thyself with Him and be at peace, thereby good shall come unto thee." So, our Lord Jesus Christ fulfilled the three essential parts of the peace offering: (1) He is the offering, (2) He is the offerer, and (3) He is the Priest—our Mediator.

1 Peter 2:24 says, "Who Himself bore our sins in His own body on the tree." 1 John 2:2 also says, "And He Himself is the Propitiation for our sins: and not for ours only, but also for the sins of the whole world." Hebrews 9:28 says, "So Christ was once offered to bear the sins of many; and unto them that look for Him shall He appear the second time without sin unto salvation."

Hebrews 10:9-14 encapsulates this message: "Then said He, Lo, I come to do thy will, O God. He taketh away the first, that He may establish the second. By which will we are sanctified through the offering of the body of Jesus Christ once for all. For by one offering He hath perfected forever them that are sanctified." Thus, the offering means that God and man are brought together in fellowship. Sin not only separated man from God but also introduced sinful actions and desires, such as hatred, unforgiveness, bitterness, and malice, among others.

Titus 3:3-6 says, "For we ourselves also were sometimes foolish, disobedient, deceived, serving diverse lusts and pleasures, living in malice and envy, hateful, and hating one another. But after that, the kindness and love of God our Savior toward man appeared...which He shed on us abundantly through Jesus Christ our Savior." This shows that our fellowship with God is brought by Christ, the Son of God, not by our works or services. It is not our successes or failures that determine our fellowship with God; rather, it is Christ. Our enjoyment of fellowship with God comes from His work accomplished for us, granting us perfect communion with our Father and our God.

The sinful nature was entirely killed and buried, and the divine nature of God was fully restored and perfectly established through the Spirit of Life in Christ Jesus now dwelling permanently in human hearts. Proverbs 4:3 says, “Guard your heart above all else, for it is the source of life” (CSB version). The NLT version of Psalm 36:9 says, “For you are the fountain of life, the light by which we see.”

Remember, all the disciples were saved through their faith in the Lord Jesus, but none of them were indwelt by the Holy Spirit because they were not yet born again, regenerated, or newly created. John 7:37-39 says, “In the last day, that great day of the feast, Jesus stood and cried saying, If any man thirst, let him come unto me and drink. He that believes on me, as the scripture hath said, out of his belly shall flow rivers of Living Water. (But this spake He of the Spirit, which they that believe on Him should receive; for the Holy Spirit was not yet given because that Jesus was not yet glorified.)" Previously, when He was physically with them, He only gave them power and sent them out to heal the sick, cast out devils, and preach. They did all these things exactly like the prophets in the Old Testament.

All the prophets in the Old Testament were saved through faith in God. None of them were born again or regenerated because they were not indwelt by the Holy Spirit. None of them had the divine nature (divine life) of God within them, including Mary, the mother of our Lord. Although the power of the Highest overshadowed her, this power was released specifically for the conception of the Son of God, the Lord Jesus, not for new creation or regeneration. Even Thomas was not regenerated, newly created, or indwelt by the Holy Spirit that Resurrection evening; because of his unbelief, he missed the first divine visitation of the Lord (John 20:24-28). Brethren, let us steadfastly believe in and constantly look unto the LORD JESUS CHRIST, the Author and Finisher of our faith. So, when did Thomas become born again, newly created, and indwelt by the Holy Spirit? We will examine this shortly.

THE NEW CREATION

Genesis 3:15 says, "And I will put enmity between thee and the woman, and between thy seed and her seed; it shall bruise thy head, and thou shalt bruise his heel."

This verse introduces two elements that were not known before in the Garden of Eden, which happens to be the foundation of Christianity. First was the curse upon mankind because of Adam's sin, and second, God's provision for a Savior who would take upon Himself the curse of sin. In summary, this means, "You will wound Him, but He will destroy you."

The "seed of the woman" refers to Jesus Christ, who was born of a woman. The enmity is between Satan and Jesus Christ. The "seed of the serpent" includes the evil men and demonic forces who struck at the heel of the Savior when Judas Iscariot, the Pharisees, and the Romans condemned Jesus to be crucified.

He was wounded, bruised, and killed for the sins of mankind, but He rose on the third day, victorious, having paid in full the penalty of sin for all who would ever believe in Him. The victory was won as He crushed the head of Satan, thereby permanently removing Satan's rule over mankind. Henceforth, Satan and all his principalities, powers, schemes, and works were destroyed. The power of the cross crushed Satan's kingdom, stripped him of his authority (particularly his power over death), and ended his tyrannical rule over mankind. By the finished work of Jesus Christ on the cross, Satan's head was crushed and defeated forever. God, being Omnipresent (All-present), Omniscient (All-knowing), and Omnipotent (All-powerful), shows us that He always had a redemption plan for mankind and informs us of His plan as soon as sin entered the world. 1 John 3:8 says, "He that committeth sin is of the devil; for the devil sinneth from the beginning. For this purpose the Son of God was manifested, that he might destroy the works of the devil."

Let's now look at the next verse, 1 John 3:9, which says, "Whosoever is born of God doth not commit sin, for His (God's) seed remaineth in him; and he cannot sin, because he is born of God."

This tells us clearly that those who are born of God (born again) do not commit sin because God's seed remains in them. In summary, the seed of the woman, Jesus Christ, has crushed the head of the serpent (the devil) and destroyed him. And verse 9 says that whoever is born of God has the seed of God in them and does not commit sin. What is the seed of God, and what about the seed of the woman?

1 Peter 1:23 says, "Being born again, not of corruptible seed, but of incorruptible, by the word of God, which liveth and abideth forever." Luke 8:11 says, "The seed is the word of God."

John 1:1 says, “In the beginning was the Word, and the Word was with God, and the Word was God.”

This simply means that any new believer in Christ is born of the incorruptible seed, which is the word of God. This is clearly stated in John 1:12-14: "But as many as received Him, to them gave He power to become the sons of God, even to them that believe on His name: which were born, not of blood, nor of the will of the flesh, nor of the will of man, but of God. And the word was made flesh, and dwelt among us, full of grace and truth."

So, as many as receive Him (Jesus Christ) as Lord and Savior and believe on His name have become sons of God by the incorruptible seed—the word of God—and by the power of God.

According to John 1:1 and 1:14 and 1 Corinthians 1:24, Jesus Christ is the Word of God, the Power of God, and the Wisdom of God. Having established this truth, let's now see how Jesus Christ made us a new creation, born of the power of God and the incorruptible word of God. In John 20:22-23, verse 22 says, "He breathed on them and saith unto them, Receive ye the Holy Spirit." But in Genesis 2:7 it is written, "And the Lord God formed man from the dust of the ground. He breathed the breath of life into the man's nostrils, and the man became a living soul."

Adam at creation became a living being with the life of God through the breath of God in him. After the fall, Adam remained humanly alive but spiritually dead—the divine nature, seed, or life of God was completely separated from Adam, leaving him with a human nature dominated by the sinful nature, also known as the Adamic nature and the old man (Romans 6:6 and 6:16).

Glory be to God! All that was symbolized at the water baptism of our Lord Jesus Christ came to fulfillment, revealing to us the redemptive order of God's righteousness for mankind. The Spirit of grace was symbolized by John, who was the forerunner and the one who was to make God the Savior, Jesus, known to sinners in the world (the wilderness). John, continuing as the spirit of grace, symbolically baptized the full man in Jesus into the full God (deity) in Jesus, symbolically in the Jordan River (the flowing river). Fulfilling this symbolism, the twelve apostles and other disciples of Jesus were called to follow Him by grace, unmerited favor, and not by their works. They were with Jesus throughout His ministry until the day He was crucified, but none of them were yet born of the Holy Spirit or newly created, including Judas, the betrayer; Peter, the denier; and Thomas, the doubter. Why? Because the Lord Jesus had not yet been crucified, not yet buried for our sins, not yet risen on the third day to give us eternal life, and not yet appeared before His Father and our Father in heaven to be glorified.

Immediately after He was crucified and rose on the third day, on that same resurrection day after He had appeared before His Father and our Father as our Firstfruit and our Peace Offering, and was glorified, He appeared to the disciples in the evening to fully fulfill the redemption order symbolized by His water baptism. He revealed Himself to them with a glorified, touchable body, not as a ghost. He released the peace of God on them, and He breathed on them, spontaneously releasing the Holy Spirit of Life in Him to them through His spoken word. At this point, exactly what had been symbolically represented at His water baptism came to fulfillment in the lives of His disciples. He literally killed the sin nature, the Adamic nature known as the "old man," within them. The disciples were born again by His Spirit of Life and became a new creation (2 Corinthians 5:16-17).

How did it happen? The divine life (nature) and divine power of God in the blood of the Lord Jesus Christ became the Spirit of Life in Christ Jesus, according to these Scriptures:

1 John 5:7-8 says, "For there are three that bear record in heaven: the Father, the Word, and the Holy Ghost; and these three are one. And there are three that bear witness in earth: the Spirit, the water, and the blood; and these three agree in one."

The Lord Jesus revealed this to us in John 3:6: "That which is born of the flesh is flesh, and that which is born of the Spirit is spirit." He clearly showed us that any believer in Christ who is born again becomes a spirit by the Spirit of Life in Christ now dwelling in us.

1 Corinthians 6:15-17 says, "Know ye not that your bodies are the members of Christ? Shall I then take the members of Christ and make them the members of a harlot? God forbid. What? Know ye not that he which is joined to a harlot is one body? For two, saith he, shall be one flesh. But he that is joined unto the Lord is one spirit."

Hebrews 9:14 says, "How much more shall the blood of Christ, who through the eternal Spirit offered Himself without spot to God, purge your conscience from dead works to serve the living God?"

Revelation 1:5 says, "And from Jesus Christ, who is the faithful witness and the first begotten of the dead, and the prince of the kings of the earth. Unto Him that loved us and washed us from our sins in His own blood."

Our Lord Jesus continues to wash sinners who accept Him as Lord and Savior. His divine life and nature in His blood is the same life of God in the Holy Spirit because the Spirit, the water, and the blood agree in one. Even medically, we have blood oxygenation, which occurs when oxygen molecules from the air we breathe enter the blood.

The Spirit of Life in Christ Jesus now in the disciples, with the divine nature and life of God, cannot coexist with the sin nature. John 1:4-5 says, "In Him (Jesus Christ) was life, and the life was the light of men. And the light shineth in darkness, and the darkness comprehended it not." The sinful nature could not understand or grasp this great power in the divine nature that had just entered, so it had to submit and surrender for its total destruction and death. "Knowing this, that our old man is crucified with Him, that the body of sin (sinful nature in mankind) might be destroyed, that henceforth we should not serve sin" (Romans 6:6). This is the same sin nature that was symbolically destroyed, dead, and flushed out of mankind, washed down by the River Jordan into the Dead Sea and buried permanently. This is the water burial of the sin nature. For confirmation, this was prophesied by the Prophet Micah in Micah 7:18-20, as mentioned in the earlier chapter. Verse 19 says, "He (God) will turn again, He will have compassion upon us; He will subdue our iniquities; and Thou wilt cast all their sins into the depths of the sea." This is why every believer, born again and newly created, has to go through water baptism after surrendering to the Lord Jesus as their Lord and Savior.

This act is not only a public declaration of faith in Jesus Christ and an outward demonstration of the inward transformation that occurs when we receive Him as Lord but also an acknowledgment that our sinful nature—the Adamic nature and old man in us—has been destroyed, dead, and undergone water burial. However, water baptism is not a requirement for salvation but a symbol of the salvation that has already taken place in our lives through accepting Jesus Christ as our Lord and Savior.

As previously stated, every believer in Christ is washed, cleansed, sanctified, and justified by the blood of Jesus and by the Spirit of our God (1 Corinthians 6:11). Romans 8:2 says, "The law of the Spirit of life in Christ Jesus has made me free from the law of sin and death." The symbolism of everything that happened in the waters of the Jordan River during Jesus' baptism was fulfilled at His crucifixion and the three days He spent in the tomb. The body of the Son of God was brutally beaten, and His sinless blood was shed for our salvation, redemption, and victory over sin, Satan, the flesh, and the world.

His coming out of the baptismal water, symbolized in His resurrection from the tomb by the power of God, was fully fulfilled in the lives of the disciples in John 20:19-23, where they became newly created and born again.

However, at this point, they were not yet sealed with the Spirit of Promise from God the Father. They were fully prepared by God the Son (the Lord Jesus) to be sealed with the Holy Spirit of Promise by God the Father, as prophesied by Joel about 800 years before its fulfillment on Pentecost. Let's now look at the descent of the Holy Spirit from heaven, the Spirit of Promise, and God's public declaration.

Matthew 3:16-4:1 says, "And Jesus, when He was baptized, went up straight out of the water. Then, Jesus was led up of the Spirit into the wilderness to be tempted by the devil." Immediately after coming out of the water, the full man in Jesus symbolized humanity, according to Romans 8:3: "For what the law could not do, in that it was weak through the flesh, God sending His own Son, in the likeness of sinful flesh, and for sin, condemned sin in the flesh." He was now a new creation, born again, with the spirit of adoption manifesting in the lives of believers, granting them freedom from the spirit of fear and filling them with power, love, and a sound mind (Romans 8:14-17; 2 Timothy 1:7).

The heavens were opened, and the Spirit of God descended upon Him. This Spirit of God is the Spirit of Promise from God the Father, which the disciples would be baptized with on Pentecost, as Jesus told them in Acts 1:4, and was confirmed when they received the Holy Spirit in the upper room, as declared by Apostle Peter in Acts 2:17. The Spirit of God here is the same Spirit of Elohim, the Creator, present at the creation of heaven and earth. The Spirit of God is the Spirit of Promise prophesied by Joel in Joel 2:28-32, which seals believers in Christ until the day of redemption (Ephesians 4:30). It was the Spirit of God that led Jesus into the wilderness, symbolizing the world, to be tempted by the devil, according to Matthew 4:1. This same Spirit of Promise was with the Lord Jesus when He fasted for 40 days and nights in the wilderness and when He was tempted by the devil.

Let's now compare all these with the events that took place after the disciples were created and became born again in John 20:19-23. They were now a new creation, born again, but they were still in the same house with the door remaining shut for another eight days according to John 20:26. Again, in John 21:2-3, as they were together, Peter said unto them, "I go a fishing." They said unto him, "We also go with thee." And that night they caught nothing. On the 40th day after His resurrection, before He ascended to heaven, the disciples being together with Him, asked Him in Acts 1:6-8, "Lord, wilt thou at this time restore again the kingdom to Israel?" And He said unto them, "It is not for you to know... and unto the uttermost part of the earth."

From these accounts, we could deduce that, although they were born again and newly created, they were still afraid, acted carnally by going back to their earlier careers of fishing, and were not yet kingdom-minded because they were concerned about the restoration of the kingdom to Israel. However, within these 40 days from His resurrection to His ascension, Lord Jesus still did many signs in their presence (John 20:30) and still focused on the things pertaining to the kingdom of God (Acts 1:3). At this point, action must follow; but who does the work?

The disciples were now newly created and born again, but they could not embark on any divine assignments because the power for action was needed. They were not capable of generating this needed power by themselves, as the assignments before each of them were spiritual and required spiritual power. This divine power belonged to God and could only be given by the Almighty God, who gives as He wills. The carrier of this divine power is God the Holy Spirit, but the giver of the power is God the Father. However, the Father gives this power only through His own Son, (God the Son, the Lord Jesus). Lord Jesus would not recommend to His Father anyone who has not met the condition of receiving this divine power. The condition is simple: Appreciate this underserved and unconditional love of God towards all humanity, then, without any procrastination, accept His Son, Lord Jesus, as your Lord and Savior. This instantly makes you ready to receive the power. Not only does God want to give us this power, but He also wants to announce to the whole world that you are His accepted, beloved, and affirmed child, anointed and ordained as king and priest to rule and to reign on the earth through His Son, Lord Jesus Christ.

Lord Jesus had given His disciples a new birth and made them a new creation by the Holy Spirit of Life in Him, but He still commanded them *not* to depart from Jerusalem until the promise of the Father, the Holy Spirit of the Promise of God, from heaven came upon them. Hence, they would receive the dynamite, the firepower needed to fulfill their individual assignments and accomplish their divine purposes of glorifying Him, both individually and collectively as children of God and as the body of Christ.

Immediately after the disciples were baptized with the Holy Spirit of God and with fire, they were labeled as those who turned the whole world upside down (Acts 17:6). This was because what they were now made up of was enormously powerful. They were born again, made a new creation by the Holy Spirit of Life in Christ Jesus, and the Spirit of Adoption, now having the divine nature and life of God in them, which prepared them to be baptized and sealed with the Spirit of Elohim, the Creator God, loaded with the power that created heaven and earth. How did they turn the world upside down?

1. Through powerful preaching and teaching: Acts 2:13-41; 3:12-26; 6:7; 12:24; 19:20.
2. Through making disciples: Acts 2:41; Acts 4:4.
3. Through powerful healings: Acts 3:1-10; Acts 5:14-16; Acts 28:8.
4. Through deliverance: Acts 16:16-18; Acts 19:11-12.
5. Through house fellowship: Acts 2:46.
6. Through converting great people: Acts 17:22-33; Acts 17:12; Acts 23:23; Acts 25:12.

HE HAS INDEED MADE US THE FINISHED PRODUCTS BY HIS FINISHED REDEMPTION WORK. GLORY BE TO GOD!!!

Immediately when a believer in Christ accepts Jesus as Lord and Savior, the Holy Spirit of Promise is readily and freely available as a gift from God the Father for us to receive by faith in Jesus Christ. Receiving the baptism of the Holy Spirit with fire can happen anywhere and anytime. You don't have to be in church or at a crusade to receive the baptism of the Holy Spirit. It could happen in your living room, bedroom, or anywhere you are worshiping Him. The only requirement is that you must be born again, created anew. God the Father wants to seal you with His Holy Spirit of Elohim, the Creator, because you have appreciated His love in giving His HOLY BELOVED SON to die for the redemption and salvation of THE WHOLE WORLD in general, and for you and me in particular. It is very important to Him, God our Father, that we are sealed with HIS SPIRIT OF PROMISE, to complete and perfect in us His new creation, orchestrated and accomplished through His Son. And we are indeed sealed according to Ephesians 4:30 until the day of redemption (the day of catching up or rapture). How? Because His Spirit of Promise comes upon us to remain with us, never to leave until the day of rapture.

Not only does He remain in us, but He also releases the power needed for each of us to accomplish our divine assignments and purposes. However, IT IS VERY IMPORTANT TO NOTE THIS: We receive the baptism with the Holy Spirit of Promise once in our lifetime because we are sealed once, but we receive His infilling with His power continuously, every day. Let's read and meditate on these four scriptures sequentially:

- John 1:33 says, "And I knew Him not, but He that sent me to baptize with water, the same said unto me, upon whom thou shalt see the Spirit descending and remaining on Him, the same is He which baptizeth with the Holy Ghost."
- Acts 1:8, "But ye shall receive power, after that the Holy Ghost is come upon you: the uttermost part of the earth."

- Acts 4:31, "And when they had prayed, the place was shaken ... and they were all FILLED with the Holy Ghost, and they spoke the word of God with boldness."
- Mark 11:24 says, "Therefore I say unto you, what things soever ye desire, when ye pray, believe that ye receive them, and ye shall have them."

Brethren, it is not only important to our Father and our God to seal (baptize) us with the Spirit of Promise and release His fire-power in us to accomplish our divine assignments and purposes, thereby fulfilling His heartbeat desire of bringing unsaved souls—if possible, ALL—into His kingdom; for He is exceedingly glorified in that. That's the reason why He laid down His life for us. It's also very important to Him that, as He symbolically announced His Son (Lord Jesus) to the world as His beloved Son coming out of the baptismal water, He has purposed to announce us, after we have surrendered ourselves to His Son, Lord Jesus, for our new creation: THAT WE ARE HIS FAVORABLY APPROVED, DEARLY LOVED CHILDREN. WE ARE THE FINISHED PRODUCTS OF HIS FINISHED REDEMPTION WORK.

Let's see again why our new creation is so spectacular to our Father and our God. God is Spirit (John 4:24), and God is love (1 John 4:16). God created angels without blood (Hebrews 1:7), but He created man with spirit, soul, and body—with blood. Unfortunately, when Adam fell into sin in the Garden of Eden, it was the blood of mankind that was infected with sin, hence, the sinful nature replaced the divine nature or life of God originally in man. "The life of the flesh is in the blood" (Leviticus 17:11).

Romans 6:6 says, "Knowing this, that our old man is crucified with Him, that the body of sin might be destroyed, that henceforth, we should not serve sin." What is this "OLD MAN"? It is the corrupt, polluted, sinful nature inherited from Adam, the first man, which ruled mankind for 4,000 years before the coming of our Lord Jesus Christ to destroy this monster and stronghold called sinful nature. It is our old self, that is, all that we were in our old unregenerate condition before union with Christ. Our Lord Jesus did the hardest part for us and left us with the simplest task of only believing in Him and what He did on the cross for us. However, as simple as He made it, it was enormously painful for His Father, our God. He was forsaken by His Father for the first time ever and never again. He was forsaken for our sakes (Matthew 27:46). God the Father knew beforehand what His beloved Son would endure for us, the filthy sinners, to be redeemed and saved. The Father, looking at His Son carrying the sins of all mankind and suffering greatly from Gethsemane to the moment He gave up His Spirit, turned against His Son because He has purer eyes and cannot behold iniquity (Habakkuk 1:13).

Hebrews 9:22 says, "Without the shedding of blood there is no remission (no forgiveness)." God loved to forgive and save us; if there had been an easier, simpler, or less strenuous way, He would have chosen it. However, He allowed it to happen because He is Love, and He loves His creation. Ephesians 2:8-9 says, "For by grace are ye saved through faith; and that not of yourselves: it is the gift of God. Not of works, lest any man should boast."

Galatians 5:6 says, "For in Jesus Christ neither circumcision availeth anything nor uncircumcision; but faith which worketh by love."

In summary, these two scriptures reveal how the Trinity has been working together for our salvation: God the Holy Spirit, the Spirit of Grace, has been working since after the resurrection of our Lord Jesus Christ, lovingly and graciously convicting mankind to bring them to God the Son, who carries out the redemption and salvation work in our lives based on His Father's love for mankind. Because He loves His Father and loves ALL MANKIND, He gave His life for us. Unfortunately, because this redemption is by grace, many people worldwide have made very little of it or treat it as unimportant. Even a few preachers treat it so lightly that, at times, when making altar calls for sinners to accept Jesus as Lord and Savior, they do so only verbally, professing without true faith from deep in their hearts. They do not believe deeply that He died and rose on the third day. Some truly confess Jesus Christ as their Lord, but because their confessions do not come from faith in what the Lord Jesus accomplished on the cross, they do not experience transformation in their lives. This is exactly what the parable of the sower reveals to us (Luke 8:4-18).

So, let us see how Lord Jesus suffered for us, why He suffered in this manner, and the purpose of His suffering for us.

Lord Jesus suffered physically, spiritually, and emotionally.

Mark 15:1 says, "And straightway in the morning the chief priests held a consultation with the elders and scribes and the WHOLE COUNCIL, and BOUND JESUS, and CARRIED HIM away, and DELIVERED him to Pilate." They took away His freedom to walk freely, and He suffered emotionally. He was bound with conspired hatred and suffered physically. Matthew 26:67 says, "Then did they spit in His face and buffeted Him; and others smote Him with the palms of their hands." Being buffeted means He was violently beaten with their fists, without any sin or offense committed against them.

Brethren, can you imagine and meditate on being spat upon, emotionally meaning being treated as a worthless person? At the same time, they hit Him violently with their anger-propelled fists, and others slapped Him hard with their hands, then mocked Him to prophesy who had hit Him. This was great torture He suffered for you and me. The sinless One suffering for the sinful, including those who were torturing Him. Brethren, pause here and witness the wickedness in mankind because of the old, sinful, Adamic nature. All this was done to Him by His brethren, even though Pontius Pilate knew they delivered Lord Jesus to him out of envy and wanted to release Him. But the chief priests and elders persuaded the multitude to ask for Barabbas, the insurrectionist, to be released and to destroy Jesus (Matthew 27:17-26).

Scourging was a painful form of torture inflicted by a whip with multiple leather cords embedded with bits of bone and sharp metal to inflict maximum pain and blood loss. Each lash would rip out large pieces of flesh, exposing skeletal muscles. All of this was done while He was still bound.

After flogging, Lord Jesus had already lost a massive amount of blood and was weak. Bleeding profusely and in severe pain, He was angrily dragged by Roman soldiers to the governor's palace, where He endured even greater humiliation and mockery. Twisting together a crown of thorns smaller than the size of His head, they forcefully rammed it onto His head and struck it with a reed, tearing flesh from His head, fresh blood running down His face. Brethren, as you read, please meditate and let your faith in Lord Jesus and all He suffered for you be viewed through the lens of His love and His Father's love for you. Imagine His sinless blood flowing out of His sinless body for sinful people and all mankind.

Now, weakened from severe blood loss and brutally battered, He was to be crucified on the cross. All of this perfectly fulfilled the prophecy of Isaiah the prophet, in Isaiah 52, about 700 years prior.

Let's look at a few scriptures revealing the atoning love of God for mankind:

Leviticus 17:11 says, "For the life of the flesh is in the blood, and I have given it to you on the altar to make atonement for your souls; for it is the blood that maketh atonement for the soul." Jesus Christ, our Lord, gave His life in His blood for us as an act of atoning love. Thank you, Lord Jesus!

Galatians 2:20 says, "I am crucified with Christ: nevertheless I live; yet not I, but Christ liveth in me; and the life which I now live in the flesh I live by the faith of the Son of God, who loved me, and gave Himself for me." Lord Jesus loved us so undeservedly and unconditionally with His agape love and gave Himself up for you and me as an act of atoning love for mankind. Now, we believers in Christ have the new life of God and His divine nature in us. Praise God!

Matthew 26:28 says, "For this is my blood of the New Testament, which is shed for many for the remission of sins." The blood of Jesus made the new covenant possible, sure, and reliable. It is confirmed with the life of God Himself, and we now have a new covenant relationship with God.

Unfortunately, many followers of Jesus live as if this never happened. Why? Because their faith is not rooted in love for the atoning sacrifice of sin He offered out of His love for us. Galatians 5:6b says, "But faith which works by love." Glory be to God! This atoning blood was not shed only for the apostles but for many who believe. Receive His life, and believe in Him. This is ALL you need.

2 Corinthians 5:21 says, "For He hath made Him to be sin for us, who knew no sin; that we might be made the right-

eousness of God in Him." By His love for us, Lord Jesus took all our sins upon Himself and released all His righteousness to us, making us the righteousness of God in Him. I love you, my Lord Jesus!

Isaiah 53:5 says, "But He was wounded for our iniquities; the chastisement of our peace was upon Him; and with His stripes we are healed." Remember, this was a prophecy of what our Lord Jesus would fulfill for us more than 700 years before His birth, and it was fulfilled accurately at His crucifixion on the cross (John 19:16-37).

The blood of Jesus is the key to abundant life, healing, deliverance, forgiveness, peace, victorious living, and hope. The full benefits of the complete redemption our Lord Jesus Christ has brought to all mankind are in His blood. Therefore, it is paramount that any believer in Christ who wishes to fully experience the power and benefit of the blood of Jesus must know the truth about the life, grace, and power in that blood to meet all their needs. Knowing the truth is not enough; one must also believe all that God's Word says about the blood of Jesus. Then, one must appropriate it by taking full advantage of the life and the enormous power in that sinless and victorious blood of Jesus. Be expectant of the manifestations of all you believe and appropriate it for, and it shall be to you according to your faith.

THE HOLY SPIRIT IN-DWELT AND CLOTHED BELIEVERS

Now that we see the roles the three Godheads played in the Redemption plan of God for mankind, it's worthwhile to go deeper into how the Holy Spirit works in us and through us. What great and deep love our Father and our God has for us through His Son, our Lord Jesus Christ, by His Spirit, the Wonderful Holy Spirit! As newly created believers in Christ, we are, according to 1 Corinthians 6:19-20:

"What? Know ye not that your body is the temple of the Holy Ghost, which is in you, which ye have of God, and ye are not your own? For ye are bought with a price; therefore glorify God in your body, and in your spirit, which are God's."

As newly created, born-again, Holy Spirit-indwelt children of God, we have been made the temple of God. How? Jesus Christ, in the person of His Holy Spirit of Life, by His power, has completely killed and buried the old man, the sinful and

Adamic nature in mankind, thus setting us free from the power of sin and death. We now have God the Father, the Creator of heaven and earth, as the Spirit of Promise dwelling in us. So, as believers in Christ, we have God Almighty, the Creator of heaven and earth, and His Beloved Son, Lord Jesus Christ, living inside us and abiding with us in the person of God the Holy Spirit. Truly, we are a new creation.

Now, having been baptized in the Jordan River, and with the Spirit of God descending upon Him like a dove, accompanied by His Father's proclamation declaring Him as His Beloved Son, Lord Jesus was led into the wilderness to be tempted by the devil (Matthew 3:17 - 4:1). He fasted for 40 days and 40 nights and was tempted by the devil with three temptations, but He defeated the devil. Then, Luke 4:13-15 says, "And when the devil had ended all the temptation, he departed from him for a season... And he taught in their synagogues, being glorified of all." Lord Jesus returned in the power of the Spirit into Galilee, and in verses 18-19 He read from the book of the prophet Isaiah (61:1-2): "The Spirit of the Lord is upon me, because He hath anointed me to preach the gospel to the poor; He hath sent me to heal the brokenhearted, to preach deliverance to the captives, and recovering of sight to the blind, to set at liberty them that are bruised, to preach the acceptable year of the Lord." Then in verse 21, He said, "This day is this scripture fulfilled in your ears."

This narrative reveals that the Spirit of the Lord is associated with great power to preach the gospel (the good news of salvation), heal the sick, set captives free, perform miracles like restoring sight to the blind, and bring comfort to those who are bruised. These are the gifts of the Holy Spirit.

Thus, as much as the Lord Jesus literally demonstrated the ministry of the gifts of the Holy Spirit in His own ministry, which was beginning at this point, He also symbolized the same pattern for us, His disciples, to follow after its fulfillment on the day of Pentecost. The Spirit of the Lord is the Spirit of Power, Freedom, Liberty, Triumph, Victory, Divine Accomplishments, and Rest, which will be established with Scriptures and examples of how various characters in the Bible operated exceedingly through Him.

However, before we examine these examples, let's see what Luke 4:14b-15 says: "And there went out a fame of Him through all the region roundabout." We are baptized with the Holy Spirit and with fire to showcase the awesomeness of God and to demonstrate the gifts and power of the Holy Spirit in people's lives all over the world by preaching and teaching with authority, healing the sick, setting captives free, and performing great miracles. Hence, bringing a great harvest of souls into the Kingdom of God. Through this, our Father is glorified by His Son, through His Holy Spirit working in and through us. Hallelujah!

Let's look at some Scriptures regarding the Spirit of the Lord and see how He worked in the lives of some heroes in the Old Testament, and also in and through the disciples from the day of Pentecost onward. The Holy Spirit worked powerfully in the lives of the disciples, enabling them to preach and teach the gospel with authority and power, heal the sick, set captives free by casting out demons, raise the dead, perform great miracles, save souls, and make disciples, thereby fulfilling their divine assignments and glorifying God.

Let's see how the Spirit of the Lord is established as the Spirit of Power, Triumph, Liberty, Victory, Divine Accomplishments, and Rest, through the following Scriptures and examples:

2 Corinthians 3:17 says, "Now the Lord is the Spirit, and where the Spirit of the Lord is, there is LIBERTY."

Isaiah 59:19 says, "So shall they fear the name of the Lord from the west, and His glory from the rising of the sun. When the enemy shall come in like a flood, the Spirit of the Lord shall lift up a standard against him."

Isaiah 63:14 says, "As a beast goes down into the valley, the Spirit of the Lord caused him to REST: so didst thou lead thy people, to make thyself a glorious name."

Judges 3:10-11 says, "And the Spirit of the Lord came upon him (Othniel, the son of Kenaz) and he judged Israel, and went out to war, and the LORD delivered...and his hand prevailed against Chushan-rishathaim. And the land had rest for forty years. And Othniel the son of Kenaz died."

Judges 6:34 says, "But the Spirit of the Lord came upon Gideon and he blew a trumpet; and Abiezer was gathered after him." Judges 8:28 says, "Thus was Midian subdued before the children of Israel, and the country was in quietness forty years in the days of Gideon."

1 Samuel 16:13 says, "Then Samuel took the horn of oil, and anointed him in the midst of his brethren; and the Spirit of the Lord came upon David..."

2 Samuel 8:1 says, "While David was King of Israel, he won many battles over the Philistines." 1 Kings 2:11 says, "And the days that David reigned over Israel were forty years - 7 years in Hebron and 33 years in Jerusalem."

In 1 Samuel 10:6, Samuel speaks to Saul: "And the Spirit of the Lord will come upon thee, and thou shalt prophesy with them, and shalt be turned into another man." This was after Saul had been anointed with oil in verse 1.

In Judges 14:6, "At that moment the Spirit of the Lord came powerfully upon him (Samson), and he ripped the lion's jaw apart with his bare hands. He did it as easily as if it were a young goat. But he did not tell his father or mother about it." (NLT)

All these heroes of faith in the Old Testament were endowed with the Spirit of the Lord for service and were used powerfully on their various assignments. However, none of them were newly created; they all had the old sinful, Adamic nature within them. They received the Spirit of the Lord either by anointing from a prophet or through angelic visitation. None of them received the anointing freely as a gift from the indwelling Holy Spirit, as they did not have the divine nature, the new Life of God within them.

Our Lord said in Matthew 13:16-17, "But blessed are your eyes, for they see; and your ears, for they hear. For verily I say unto you, that many prophets and righteous men have desired to see those things which ye see, and have not seen them; and to hear those things which ye hear, and have not heard them." In other words, they longed to experience what we now freely receive.

In corroboration, the Apostle Peter said in 1 Peter 1:10-12, "Of which salvation the prophets have inquired and searched diligently, who prophesied of the grace that should come unto you... which things the angels desire to look into."

Apostle Paul spends the entire 2 Corinthians 3 contrasting the new and old covenants. In verses 17-18, he writes, "Now the Lord is the Spirit; and where the Spirit of the Lord is, there is liberty. But we all, with open face beholding as in a glass the glory of the Lord, are changed into the same image from glory to glory, even as by the Spirit of the Lord."

This means that the freedom of the Spirit of the Lord liberates believers in Jesus Christ from the constraints of the law and bestows upon them the glory of the new covenant.

So, in summary, the Spirit of the Lord, whom the heroes of the Old Testament received through angelic visitation or prophetic anointing, is now freely given to those born again through the blood of the new covenant, shed on the Cross of

Calvary. As believers in Christ Jesus, born again by the Spirit of Life, with the divine nature and Life of God in us, we are fully freed from the spirit of fear. We are now endowed with power, love, and a sound mind by the Holy Spirit of adoption (Romans 8:14-17 and 2 Timothy 1:7). Sealed until the day of redemption and fully baptized with the Spirit of God and with divine fire, WE NOW RECEIVE AND ARE COMPLETELY AND FREELY CLOTHED WITH THE FULL PRESENCE OF THE SPIRIT OF THE LORD.

A FINAL NOTE

Having seen the foreshadowing, the symbolism, and the fulfillment of God's redemption plan for mankind, we turn to John 8:32, which says, "And ye shall know the truth, and the truth shall make you free." The truth about God's entire plan of righteousness and redemption for mankind is for all believers in Christ Jesus to know WHO WE ARE IN GOD—not what we are trying to be through our own efforts, but what the Trinity has planned from the foundation of the earth (Ephesians 1:4-5). This plan was symbolized (personified, embodied, illustrated, or typified) to guide all believers in Christ to follow after it was fulfilled by the Lord Jesus.

1 Corinthians 5:16-17 says, "Wherefore henceforth know we no man after the flesh: yea, though we have known Christ after the flesh, yet now henceforth know we him no more. Therefore if any man be in Christ, he is a new creature (new

creation): old things are passed away: behold, all things have become new. And all things are of God, who has reconciled us to Himself by Jesus Christ, and has given to us the ministry of reconciliation."

The fact is that every product contains its components to a greater or lesser extent, which are what the consumer uses when evaluating alternatives. For example, a ring or necklace made of gold is different in quality and value from one made of silver. Likewise, according to the word of our Lord Jesus Christ—the Truth Himself—in John 3:5-6, "Jesus answered, Verily, verily, I say unto thee, Except a man be born of water and of the Spirit, he cannot enter into the kingdom of God. That which is born of the flesh is flesh; and that which is born of the Spirit is spirit."

Romans 8:8-10 states, "So then they that are in the flesh cannot please God. But ye are not in the flesh, but in the Spirit, if so be that the Spirit of God dwells in you. Now if any man has not the Spirit of Christ, he is none of his. And if CHRIST BE IN YOU, the body is dead because of sin; but the Spirit is life because of righteousness."

Unfortunately, many children of God, newly created, born-again believers in Christ Jesus, do not look at themselves through the mirror of God's truthful word. Despite what the Trinity has done and revealed to us, many believers in Christ have not recognized their true identity or who they are in Christ. Many accurately and frequently confess that they are new creations in Christ Jesus, but their confessions may not yet be rooted in faith in God, or they may not fully understand the REALITY and truth upon which their confessions are based. This book seeks to address this through divine revelation by the Holy Spirit.

John 16:13 says, "Howbeit when He, the Spirit of Truth, is come, He will guide you into all truth; for He shall not speak of Himself: but whatsoever He shall hear, that shall He speak: and He will shew you things to come."

This is a true revelation of the truth that has been symbolized, carried out, and fulfilled for us to know, believe, actualize as truth, and live as children of God. Brethren, let's stop downplaying or diminishing what the Son of God, Lord Jesus Christ, laid down HIS LIFE for us to become in Him. Now, as believers in Christ and children of the Living God, we LITERALLY, TRULY, ACTUALLY, PRECISELY HAVE GOD THE FATHER, GOD THE SON, IN THE PERSON OF GOD THE HOLY SPIRIT, DWELLING IN US AND ABIDING WITH US. This redemption plan and order for all believers to follow was foreshadowed in the Old Testament by God the Father; it was symbolized at water baptism by God the Son, Lord Jesus Christ; and literally fulfilled and actualized first in the disciples on His resurrection day by God the Son and God the Holy Spirit in John 20.

Apostle Paul, reminding us who we are in Christ Jesus, said in 1 Corinthians 6:19-20, "What? Know ye not that your body is the temple of the Holy Ghost which is in you, WHICH YE HAVE OF GOD, and ye are not your own? For ye are

BOUGHT WITH A PRICE: therefore glorify God in your body and in your spirit, which are God's."

In the same way that we buy new clothes, put them on, and admire ourselves in a mirror, let us begin to look at ourselves in the mirror of God's word. Let's see how qualitatively valuable and beautiful we have been made to be and to appear. How did this happen? By our good works or service to God? NO! We are bought with a price, not by our own payment. And how? With something imperishable, incomparable to any commonly agreed, most valuable, and most durable thing in the entire universe. 1 Peter 1:18-19 says, "Forasmuch as ye know that ye were not redeemed with corruptible things, as silver and gold, from your vain conversation received by tradition from your fathers, but with the precious blood of Christ, as of a lamb without blemish and without spot."

The precious blood of Jesus contains the life of Jesus Christ. This life is the divine life of God called the Spirit of Life. Believe this truth, meditate on it, and live it by walking in it, now that you and I are born again and newly created. We have the life of Christ, God the Son, in us. How? In the person of God, the Holy Spirit of Life. This clearly and truthfully means that you and I have ALL AND EVERYTHING in the LIFE OF JESUS within us. Just as the Word of Truth says in Leviticus 17:11, "For the life of the flesh is in the blood: and I have given it to you upon the altar to make an atonement for your souls; for it is the blood that makes an atonement for the soul." Now, pause, meditate, and believe this truth: As a new creation, born again, and indwelt by the Spirit of Life in

Christ, we have ALL things associated with the life of Jesus Christ, the Son of the Living God, within us. 2 Peter 1:3 says, "His divine power has granted to us all things that pertain to life and godliness, through the knowledge of him who called us to his own glory and excellence."

The Life of Christ is simply the character of God, which is collectively the Fruit of the Spirit. Galatians 5:19-24 clearly reveals and differentiates the sinful acts called the works of the flesh from the Fruit of the Spirit. Verses 22-23 state, "But the fruit of the Spirit is love, joy, peace, long-suffering, gentleness, goodness, faith, meekness, temperance (self-control): against such there is no law." However, if we study those sinful acts from verses 19-21 carefully, we can conclude how terrible unregenerate, sin-natured humanity is. Verses 19-21 say, "Now the works of the flesh are manifest, which are these: adultery, fornication, uncleanness... they which do such things shall not inherit the kingdom of God."

Glory be to God, our Father, who in His love for us reveals and differentiates the offspring of the old man, the Adamic, sinful nature, which controls the lives of disobedient and proud people who reject the calling of God's love to repentance and surrender to the Lordship of Jesus Christ, the Savior of the whole world, and the ONLY WAY to the Kingdom of God.

Dear brothers and sisters, if you are reading this and have not yet submitted your life to Jesus Christ as your Lord and Savior, the door of mercy is still open, and amazing grace beckons you to come to NEW ABUNDANT LIFE IN THE KINGDOM OF GOD. If you are ready, please repeat after me:

"Lord Jesus, the Son of the Living God, I thank You for Your undeserved and unconditional love for the whole world in general and for me in particular. I acknowledge myself as a sinner, urgently in need of You, the Savior of the world. I repent of all my sins and surrender my life to You now. I confess You as my Lord and my Savior, for I believe with all my heart that You died for me on the Cross of Calvary, took my sins away, and rose on the third day to give me everlasting life in Your Kingdom. Thank You, Lord Jesus, for I am now born again, newly created, and indwelt with Your Holy Spirit. In Jesus' name, Amen."

PRAISE GOD! CONGRATULATIONS AND WELCOME TO ABUNDANT AND ETERNAL LIFE IN CHRIST. The angels in heaven are rejoicing because of your new life in Christ. GLORY TO THE LORD! HALLELUJAH!

Now, to all newly created, born-again children of God, we have been given power by the Spirit of Life in Christ to set us free from the power of sin and death. Therefore, we must appropriate this power every day in our prayers, seeking the overflowing manifestation of the Fruit of the Holy Spirit—the character of God—in our lives, and the continuous destruction of any work of the flesh that may try to arise.

If you need deliverance from any bondage, yoke, oppression, depression, sickness, or temptation, please pray this prayer with complete faith in our Lord Jesus Christ and belief in all He has accomplished for you on the Cross of Calvary:

"Father, in the gracious name of Jesus, by my hope and trust in You, my Father, and by my faith in You, my Lord Jesus, and Your victorious blood shed on the Cross of Calvary; by the fire, power, and authority of the Holy Spirit, my Helper, I break and destroy every infirmity in any area of my body and every form of bondage (name specific areas of need). I declare these broken and destroyed now. I receive my healing and my deliverance in Jesus' mighty and powerful name. Amen."

Now, ask for the exceeding and overflowing manifestation of the nine fruits of the Holy Spirit, mentioning each one in Jesus' name. Amen.

Brethren, consider what the Holy Spirit has revealed to us and how much more He desires to reveal. Reflect on this love that God, our Father, has shown us by giving His only begotten Son to come to this sinful world and die for the sin (the Adamic nature) in mankind. He is Love, and He loves us immeasurably. He constantly loves us, and nothing we do can add to or reduce His love. Because He is Love, He desires His children to love Him completely. That is why He gave His only begotten Son so that, by accepting Him as our Lord and Savior, His Holy Spirit would dwell within us and pour His love into our hearts (Romans 5:5), enabling us to love Him with all our heart, soul, mind, and strength and to love one another as ourselves (Matthew 22:37-40). This tells us that God, our Father, wants us to love Him with all that

He has made us to be through His beloved Son and by His Spirit.

Father, from the depths of our hearts, we say we love You with all our hearts, with all our souls, with all our minds, and with all our strength. We worship and adore You every moment of our lives in Jesus' mighty name. And our Lord Jesus, the Son of God, finds great joy when we love one another, as He said in John 13:34-35, "A new commandment I give unto you, that ye love one another; as I have loved you, that ye also love one another. By this shall all men know that ye are my disciples, if ye have love one to another." The Holy Spirit receives honor when we work together in unity and love, as shown in Acts 4:32: "All the believers were united in heart and mind. And they felt that what they owned was not their own, so they shared everything they had."

Let's look further at the enormous benefits of what the Lord Jesus did for us through His death and resurrection. When we accept Him as our Lord and personal Savior, becoming born again and a new creation, the Holy Spirit, as the Spirit of Grace (John 1:16), manifests exceedingly in our lives, allowing us to receive grace upon grace by the fullness of Jesus. We also receive the following benefits and enjoy them in our lives by His fullness: adoption as sons of God into the family of God (Romans 8:14-15), the glory of the Lord radiating upon us (Isaiah 61:1-2 and 1 Peter 4:14). According to Isaiah 11:1-2, "And there shall come forth a rod out of the stem of Jesse, and a branch shall grow out of his roots: And the Spirit of the Lord shall rest upon Him, the Spirit of wisdom and understanding, the Spirit of counsel and might, the Spirit of knowledge and of the fear of the Lord."

Lord Jesus is the Way, the Truth, and the Life; He enters our lives and releases His truth freely through the Spirit of Truth (John 14:17). He also brings comfort through the Holy Spirit as our Comforter (John 14:16) so that He may abide with us forever.

Having seen the great and marvelous works our Lord Jesus accomplished for us at the stage of creating us anew and making us born again with all the accompanying benefits, let's move to the next stage in God's Redemption Plan for humanity. The Holy Spirit of Grace has baptized us into the body of the Lord Jesus Christ, and the Spirit of Life has given us a new birth. We are now a new creation with the divine life of Christ in us, along with tremendous benefits. This stage corresponds to the symbolism of the water baptism of Jesus, marking the point when He emerged from the Jordan River; it is also the same point when Jesus appeared to the disciples in the evening on the day of His resurrection. They became newly created and born again after He breathed on them and released the Holy Spirit of Life into them.

Thus, any new believer in Christ who is born again and newly created, as symbolized at water baptism and fulfilled in the disciples on the resurrection evening, is now prepared and ready to be SEALED with the Holy Spirit of Promise from God the Father, who seals us until the day of redemption.

This Holy Spirit of Promise is the same Spirit of God, Elohim, the Creator of heaven and earth.

The word "seal" in the dictionary means a device or substance used to join two things together, preventing them from coming apart or allowing anything to pass between them. The Oxford English Dictionary defines "seal" as a token or symbol of a covenant; something that authenticates, confirms, or secures as a final addition.

From the previous chapters, we know that the Spirit of God, as the Spirit of Promise from the Father and the Spirit of Elohim, does not only seal a newly created, born-again believer in Christ until the day of redemption, but He also descends on that believer with an accompanying voice of great announcement—of acceptance, affection, and affirmation—from God Almighty, the Elohim, the monotheistic Creator seated on His glorious throne in the heaven of heavens (Psalm 115:3).

Reflecting on the Oxford English Dictionary's meaning of "seal" as a token or symbol of a covenant that authenticates or confirms something as a final addition to join two things together, we can see the spiritual power of the word "seal" and understand its deeper meaning.

This seal, in essence, shows that God the Father, God the Son, and God the Holy Spirit work together as the Trinity in the new creation of those who believe in Jesus and accept Him as their Lord and Savior. The Son of the living God, Lord Jesus, completed His work of transforming sinful humanity into born-again, Holy Spirit-indwelt new creations with enormous corresponding benefits. However, these newly created believers need to be sealed with the covenant seal of the Holy Spirit of Promise, descending directly from God the Father in heaven.

Therefore, God the Son, Jesus Christ, who indwells the newly created, born-again believer, is now BONDED together with God the Father, Elohim, the Creator, through the covenant seal of God the Holy Spirit of Promise. This fulfills the words of Jesus in His dialogue with Nicodemus in John 3:1-21. Specifically, verses 5 and 6 state, "Jesus answered, 'Verily, verily, I say unto thee, except a man be born of water and of the Spirit, he cannot enter into the Kingdom of God. That which is born of the flesh is flesh, and that which is born of the Spirit is spirit.'" The Holy Spirit of Promise from God the Father seals every newly created, born-again believer with the COVENANT BOND of the Father, Son, and Holy Spirit until the day of redemption, the day of rapture.

After being sealed, there was a loud voice of authentication and confirmation from God the Father, seated on His highly exalted, glorious throne in heaven, announcing His acceptance, affection, and affirmation of every newly created believer. This was precisely what happened on the day of Pentecost in Jerusalem about 2000 years ago, as recorded in Acts 2:6: "Now when this was noised abroad, the multitude came together, and were confounded, because that every man heard them speak in his own language."

All the disciples were already born again and newly created, with God the Son, in the person of the Holy Spirit of Life, fully dwelling in them. They were ready for the Holy Spirit of Promise from God the Father to baptize them with fire in the upper room that day of Pentecost. The question is: When did the other disciples in the upper room on Pentecost, who were not yet breathed upon by Jesus, become born again and newly created?

When Jesus breathed on them, He gave them authority to remit and retain sin (John 20:22-23). During the ten days they spent together in the upper room before the Holy Spirit's arrival, they were united in prayer. Peter likely led them in repenting of their sins, for they had been with the Lord for 3½ years and understood the importance of repentance. Moreover, they now had authority to remit or retain sin, which they had never been given before. As Jews, they knew that only God could forgive sins. They had witnessed Jesus forgiving sins during His ministry and were convinced that He was the Son of God. It is reasonable to believe that Peter and the other already born-again disciples led the others in prayers of repentance, or that Jesus Himself may have remitted their sins during the 40 days before His ascension, as John 20:30-31 states that He performed many signs in their presence.

Another important question for many believers is: Does a newly created, born-again believer in Christ need to be sealed with the Holy Spirit of Promise from the Father, which is the same as being baptized with the Holy Spirit and with fire?

The answer is, of course, yes! This is one of the reasons why the baptism of our Lord Jesus was symbolized and literalized.

Brethren, this is the Redemption plan of God, orderly laid down for us to follow in order to fulfill our individual divine purposes. For this reason, His Redemption plan was symbolized and literalized by Lord Jesus Himself. If a believer chooses not to be baptized with the Holy Spirit and fire, he or she would still be raptured and could live a victorious Christian life, as the divine power in the blood of Jesus has completely killed the sin nature at the point of salvation or regeneration. The divine nature, the Life of God with the great power of the Spirit of Life in Christ, is now present in them. However, such believers may encounter more temptations, more oppression, and more opposition than those who are sealed or baptized with the Holy Spirit. Being baptized with the Holy Spirit not only authenticates and announces us as accepted, loved, verified, and approved children of God, but it also serves as a covenant seal that acts as a Restrainer against attacks from Satan and his agents. Brethren, the sealing or baptism with the Holy Spirit and fire not only releases power but also comes with fire, often referred to as firepower or dynamite.

Let's now examine the characteristics and benefits of the Spirit of God, the Spirit of Elohim, the Creator God, with whom we are baptized and endowed with fire. Having seen the tremendous benefits and power we are given through our new creation by the Lord Jesus Christ, the Son of the Living God, let's look at what the Spirit of God the Father (the Spirit of Elohim, Creator of heaven and earth) has endowed us with as newly created, born-again children of God. The Spirit of God was present with God the Father and God the Son (the Word) at the beginning of creation (Genesis 1:1-31). Thus, the Spirit of God within us carries great creative ability and authority to bring forth new things if we truly know and believe in the finished work that has made us who we are in CHRIST JESUS, rather than what we attempt to become by our own efforts, which often result in struggle. At the creation of heaven and earth, it was the Spirit of God who hovered over the waters, wielding awesome power by which the universe was created from nothing. This is the very power within us as new creations, born-again children of God.

The Spirit of God not only endows us with creative ability and awesome power but also fills us with wisdom, knowledge, and understanding. Proverbs 3:19-20 states, "The Lord by wisdom founded the earth; by understanding He established the heavens. By knowledge the depths are broken up, and the clouds drop down the dew." This same wisdom, understanding, and knowledge are brought to us, newly born believers in Christ, through the Spirit of God.

Let's look at Exodus 31:1-4 to see how this operates in us: "And the LORD spoke to Moses, saying, 'See, I have called by name Bezalel the son of Uri, the son of Hur, of the tribe of Judah; and I have filled him with the Spirit of God, in wisdom, in understanding, in knowledge, and in all manner of workmanship, to devise skillful works, to work in gold, silver, and bronze.'" Here's the key point: God knows each person He created on earth by name, even down to their origin. He has given each one a specific assignment to fulfill, with the divine purpose of glorifying Him. Bezalel, the son of Uri, was known by God, filled with His Spirit, and given wisdom, understanding, and knowledge in all manner of craftsmanship. These were all that Bezalel needed to fulfill his God-given assignment and, in doing so, he glorified God by accomplishing his divine purpose.

Bezalel was filled with the Spirit of God in wisdom, understanding, and knowledge because he was part of God's people under the covenant with Abraham, though he was not born again. They were saved by faith, as our Lord Jesus had not yet come to bring about the new creation. Now that we are newly created and born again through the Spirit of Life in Christ BY THE BLOOD OF JESUS, we are not only filled with the Spirit of God, but we are made of the Spirit of God (the Spirit of Elohim, Creator God) and the Spirit of Life in Christ (Lord Jesus).

This is WHO WE ARE, with the divine life of Jesus Christ within us, sealed with the covenant seal of the Spirit of Promise from God the Father, Elohim, Creator God, and equipped with various abilities needed to fulfill His divine assignments for our lives, thereby accomplishing our divine purpose of glorifying Him. One more significant ability we are endowed with is the power to prophesy—to speak with power, authority, and boldness. This spoken power and authority, through which heaven and earth were created, allows us to fulfill our Father's will, thus glorifying Him and accomplishing our divine purpose.

In conclusion, brethren, it is of utmost importance and necessity for all born-again, newly created believers in Christ to be sealed (baptized) with the COVENANT SEAL of the Spirit of Promise of Elohim, the Creator God, and with fire, so we can bring the billions of unsaved souls into the Kingdom, glorifying our Lord Jesus throughout the world.

We have been made a new creation with a new birth by the Holy Spirit of Life in Christ Jesus and the Spirit of Adoption, orchestrated by the precious, sinless, and powerful Blood of Jesus Christ, shed on the Cross of Calvary for us. Being baptized and sealed with the Spirit of Promise from God, the Spirit of Elohim, Creator of heaven and earth, we are supernaturally clothed with the Spirit of the Lord.

As discussed in the previous chapter, this Spirit brings liberty, freedom, victory, triumph, rest, peace, conquest, and longevity. He anoints us with awesome power and the great gifts we need to fulfill our individual and collective assignments, glorifying Him across the earth. PRAISE GOD!!!

HIS LAST WORD ON THE CROSS WAS:

IT IS FINISHED.

WE ARE HIS FINISHED PRODUCTS!!!

I AM THE FINISHED PRODUCT OF HIS FINISHED REDEMPTION WORK!!!

Therefore, dear brothers and sisters, if you are ready to receive this freely given gift of the wonderful and powerful Spirit of God, please pray this prayer along with me, and you shall become His finished product.

Heavenly Father, in the Name of Your Son Jesus Christ and by the Power and Authority of Your Holy Spirit, I thank You from the depths of my heart for Your love toward all people You have created, especially toward me. By this revelation of Your wonderful Redemption plan for me, by my trust in You, my Father, and my faith in Your Son, my Lord and Savior Jesus Christ, I now receive Your wonderful and powerful free gift of Your Holy Spirit of Promise. Baptize me now with fire in Jesus' gracious and glorious Name. I receive Him now, and I have Him now, in Jesus' Name (Amen).

www.ingramcontent.com/pod-product-compliance
Lightning Source LLC
LaVergne TN
LVHW050558160826
845677LV00011B/2356

* 9 7 9 8 8 9 5 6 9 7 2 1 4 *